DATE DUE

~~DE 19~~			
NO 1 1 '08			

DEMCO 38-296

ANCIENT PEOPLE OF THE ARCTIC

Robert McGhee

A N C I E N T

P E O P L E

O F   T H E

A R C T I C

UBC PRESS / VANCOUVER

PUBLISHED IN ASSOCIATION WITH THE
CANADIAN MUSEUM OF CIVILIZATION

Canadian Cataloguing in Publication Data

McGhee, Robert, 1941-
        Ancient people of the Arctic

        Includes bibliographical references and index.
        ISBN 0-7748-0553-6 (bound). – ISBN 0-7748-0631-1 (pbk.)

        1. Paleo-Indians – Canada, Northern – Antiquities. 2. Archaeology – Canada, Northern.
3. Canada, Northern – Antiquities. I. Title.

E99.E7M333 1996   971.9'01   c96-910264-x

UBC Press gratefully acknowledges the ongoing support to its publishing program from the Canada
Council, the Province of British Columbia Cultural Services Branch, and the Department of
Communications of the Government of Canada.

Set in Columbus and Foundry Sans
Printed and bound in Canada by Friesens
Copy-editor: Camilla Jenkins
Designer: George Vaitkunas
Indexer: Robert Glen
Proofreader: Barbara Tessman

UBC Press
University of British Columbia
6344 Memorial Road
Vancouver, BC V6T 1Z2
(604) 822-3259
Fax: 1-800-668-0821
E-mail: orders@ubcpress.ubc.ca
http://www.ubcpress.ubc.ca

Contents

Maps, Figures, and Illustrations

Colour plates following page 148

Acknowledgments

The archaeological evidence on which this book is based has accumulated over the past half-century, through the work of several dozen archaeologists. My personal knowledge comes largely from scavenging their reports, from listening to them describe their findings, and from asking them questions. I thank them for their generosity and for the photographs they have provided for this book, and beg their forgiveness for using their information to support interpretations with which they would not agree. A number of archaeologists have worked with me in the Arctic, and I owe each of them a debt of gratitude for their work, companionship, and acceptance of living conditions that were at times thoroughly uncomfortable. Of these, Dale Russell deserves special recognition for the many summers when we shared a tent, for his outstanding abilities to discover the most minimal traces of ancient occupation, and for his enthusiasm in trying to understand the Palaeo-Eskimos as humans. My Arctic fieldwork has been funded over the years by the Canadian Museum of Civilization and by grants from the Social Sciences and Humanities Research Council and from Cominco Ltd. For the past quarter-century this research, and that of most of my colleagues, has been possible only through the support of the Polar Continental Shelf Project, which provides logistic support to researchers throughout the Arctic Archipelago. I can speak on behalf of all Arctic archaeologists in stating our gratitude to this outstanding organization and to its pilots, who not only carry us to our work but often find it for us. The personnel of the PCSP base at Resolute Bay, and indeed all of the people of that community, deserve special thanks.

The production of the book gave me the pleasure of dealing with some very talented people. At the Canadian Museum of Civilization, Harry Foster took the superb photographs of artifacts, and Cathrine Wanczycki shepherded the book through the publication process. At UBC Press, Camilla Jenkins was a splendid and congenial editor, and George Vaitkunas not only designed the book but produced engaging maps and charts from my very sketchy originals. Finally, I wish to express my gratitude to Patricia Sutherland, who over the years has helped me immeasurably; as co-curator of the exhibition *Lost Visions, Forgotten Dreams,* she has stimulated the efforts and shared the trials involved in writing this book.

Illustration credits

Photographs by Harry Foster, with the permission of the Canadian Museum of Civilization: all colour plates following p. 148; pp. 15, *bottom,* 27, 28, 36, 109, *top,* 132, 141, 143, *bottom,* 153, 163, 165, 169, 182, 205, 225. Artifacts shown in Plate 5 are from the Parks Canada collection. Paintings by Francis Back, photographed by Harry Foster, with the permission of the Canadian Museum of Civilization: pp. 56-7, 63. Photographs by Robert McGhee: pp. 4, 19, *bottom,* 21, 35, 38, *top,* 42, 68, 69, 74-5, 79, 82-3, 90-1, 94-5, 100-1, 112-13, 133, 151, 180-1, 185, 186-7, 192-3, 208-9, 212, 214-15, 216-17, 219, 227. Photographs by Patricia Sutherland: pp. 46, *top,* 49, 51, 52, 139, 143, *top.* Others: p. 14, From the Department of Prints and Drawings of the Zentralbibliothek Zürich; p. 15, *top,* H.H. Houben, *Der Ruf des Nordens* (Berlin: Frundsbergvorlag 1927); p. 19, *top,* photograph by Jacques Cinq-Mars; pp. 26, *top,* Canadian Museum of Civilization 51167; p. 26, *bottom,* Canadian Museum of Civilization 50806; p. 38, *bottom,* Knud Leem, *Beskrivelse Over Finmarkens Lapper* (Copenhagen: G.G. Galifarb 1767); p. 43, O.V. Kotzebue, *A Voyage of Discovery into the South Sea and Beerings Straits, for the Purpose of Exploring a North-East Passage, Undertaken in the Years 1815-1818* (London: Longman, Hurst, Reese, Orme and Brown 1821); p. 46, *bottom,* photograph by David Gray; p. 53, Canadian Museum of Civilization 39037; p. 86-7, photograph by Raymond LeBlanc; p. 109, *bottom,* photograph by David Fisher; p. 127, Canadian Museum of Civilization 39054; p. 137, W.E. Parry, *Journal of a Second Voyage for the Discovery of the Northwest Passage ... in the years 1821-22-23* (London: John Murray 1824); p. 176, painting by Major George Seton, National Archives Canada, Ottawa, C-1063; p. 198-9,

Canadian Museum of Civilization 37081; p. 222, Louis Choris, *Voyage Pittoresque Autour du Monde* (Paris: Firmin Didot 1822); p. 224, Canadian Museum of Civilization G.S. 2239

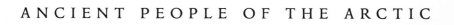

ANCIENT PEOPLE OF THE ARCTIC

CHAPTER 1

A People of the Imagination

We live in a world with no new horizons. Every patch of the globe's surface is scanned by satellite-borne instruments, while submarines rummage about in the deepest oceans. Our machines allow us to visit most regions of the earth in security and comfort. Space probes and telescopes investigate the farthest reaches of the universe, and the geographical mysteries of our world are becoming continuously more remote.

One region that our technology has not yet breached is the past. The past is as much a part of the human experience as any remote part of the earth. It is the region where all of our ancestors once lived and where they developed the cultures and traditions on which we base our present ways of life. We are all immigrants from the past, from a shadowy homeland to which we can never return.

Visiting the Past

We have relatively secure lines of communication into those portions of the past that were recorded by written history or by remembered oral tradition, but news from more distant regions reaches us rarely and is usually vague or confused. We hear of strange peoples, forgotten customs, and lost civilizations. The messengers bearing this news are generally archaeologists, and their messages are not firsthand reports passed on to us by the occupants of these distant regions. Rather, they are the accounts of witnesses who have made fleeting visits into the past and have never encountered its occupants, although they have seen fragments of their settlements. At best, archaeologists can report that they have visited a

This tiny arrowpoint, meticulously chipped
from pink flint, has lain on an Arctic beach
for 4,000 years.

deserted house, a corner of the wall surrounding an abandoned city, a graveyard after the mourners have departed, or the remains of a hunters' camp after its occupants have moved on. From what they saw and what they can learn from the tokens they have picked up from these ancient sites, they sketch travellers' tales of remote worlds and alien peoples.

Most of the ancient cultures delineated by archaeologists are similar to ones that we know from historical depictions or from the descriptions of travellers who have lived among distant peoples in the present world. Reports from the tombs of ancient Egyptians generally confirm what we know of these people from the written testimony of the Greeks, Hebrews, and other early Mediterranean peoples. We are not surprised to learn that the people who built Stonehenge probably had a political organization similar to that of the sixteenth-century Cherokee, a nation that also built massive ceremonial structures. The remains of a thousand-year-old agricultural village on the shores of the Great Lakes suggest a society and economy already known to us through the historical Iroquois, as well as through the northern Europeans described in the story of Beowulf.

Occasionally, however, archaeologists come upon remains that seem to depict a way of life outside the range of known human experience. However they combine their pieces of evidence, the picture that emerges does not resemble anything known from elsewhere in the past or present world. The first occupants of the New World Arctic are such a case.

A Singular People

Arctic North America has long been the homeland of the people known to Europeans as Eskimos. The name 'Eskimo' has recently been partially replaced by the name 'Inuit,' especially among the Arctic peoples of Canada and Greenland from whose language the term comes. But the much larger populations of closely related peoples occupying Alaska and eastern Siberia still refer to themselves as Eskimos, and the term is useful in referring to the broad range of Arctic peoples speaking languages of the Eskimo family. 'Inuit' is more commonly used to designate the eastern branch of the population, occupying the Arctic coasts from Bering Strait to Greenland.

For over half a century, archaeologists have known that human groups had occupied the barren tundra regions of Arctic North America prior to the arrival of ancestral Inuit. From Alaska to Greenland, they reported the remains of small settlements containing the ruins of structures built to

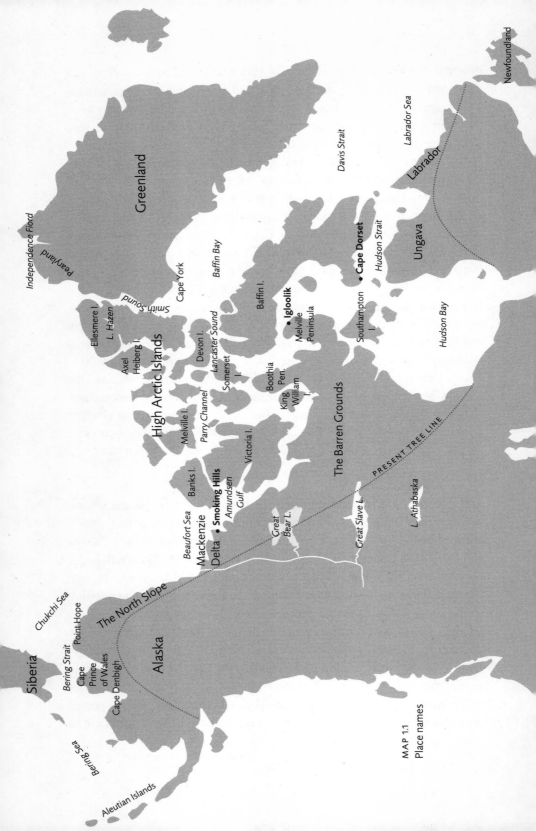

Siberia

Bering Sea

Aleutian Islands

Cape Denbigh
Cape Prince of Wales
Bering Strait
Point Hope
Chukchi Sea

Alaska

The North Slope

Beaufort Sea

Mackenzie Delta
Smoking Hills
Amundsen Gulf

Banks I.

Melville I.

Parry Channel

Victoria I.

Great Bear L.

Great Slave L.

L. Athabaska

The Barren Grounds

PRESENT TREE LINE

High Arctic Islands

Ellesmere I.
L. Hazen
Axel Heiberg I.
Devon I.
Somerset I.
King William I.
Boothia Pen.

Lancaster Sound

Baffin I.

Igloolik
Melville Peninsula

Baffin Bay

Cape York

Smith Sound

Greenland

Independence Fiord

Peary/and

Davis Strait

Labrador Sea

Newfoundland

Labrador

Ungava

Hudson Strait

Cape Dorset

Southampton I.

Hudson Bay

MAP 1.1
Place names

distinctly non-Inuit patterns. From these sites came tiny artifacts, manu-factured with techniques and styles markedly different from those used by the Inuit of later times.

Archaeologists referred to the people who left these singular remains as Palaeo-Eskimos – Old Eskimos – simply because they lived in the environment later occupied by Eskimo peoples. Despite the name, however, archaeologists had to admit that they did not know whether the Palaeo-Eskimos were in any way related to the Eskimos or Inuit of the present world. In fact, the more Palaeo-Eskimo settlements excavated and the more collections examined, the more unusual did the people who left these remains appear.

It gradually became apparent that the Inuit way of life could not be used as a model to interpret the culture, economy, or social organiza-tion of this earlier group. Archaeology was deprived of one of its favourite tools for reconstructing the life styles of ancient peoples: extending the culture of an historically known group backwards into time in order to explain the archaeological remains of their ancestors. In the Palaeo-Eskimos, archaeologists had encountered a group without clear descen-dants in the recorded world. Moreover, their way of life appeared to show little resemblance to that of any other people known to history or anthro-pology. If the Palaeo-Eskimos were to be understood, it would have to be on the basis of archaeology alone.

Archaeology in a Cold Climate

The Arctic, however, is kind to archaeologists. Cold and dry weather, the defining characteristic of the Arctic environment, produces conditions that well preserve the relics of past events. Geological processes, which shape the landscape, work at a much slower rate in Arctic regions than they do elsewhere. For most of the year the land is locked in ice, and the light summer rainfalls rarely produce eroding torrents or silt-laden floods. When archaeologists visit an ancient rivermouth camp, a hilltop lookout, or a hunting station perched on a gravel terrace above the coast, the sur-face they tread is the same one on which the Palaeo-Eskimo people lived thousands of years before. The local scenery has not changed over the intervening centuries. The archaeologist needs little imagination to picture the appearance of the ancient settlement or to guess why the people picked this location in which to live.

The same conditions ensure that biological changes to the landscape also occur very slowly. No forests have grown to hide the sites of Palaeo-Eskimo settlements, and in many regions the hearths and bone dumps and lost artifacts are not even hidden by layers of turf or humus. Tools and weapons lie where they were lost in the snow or the darkness of a winter night hundreds or thousands of years ago. Simply scanning the surface of a Palaeo-Eskimo site, an archaeologist sees the settlement very much as it looked the day after its inhabitants had moved away for the last time.

Most remarkable is the preservation of artifacts that have lain abandoned since their owners left. Stone tools, of course, are the most resistant to damage or deterioration; stone artifacts that were made and then lost thousands of years ago would be perfectly useful today as tips for weapons or blades for knives. In most parts of the world, artifacts such as these are all that is left from the technology of Stone Age peoples; the vast majority of their artifacts, made from wood and fibre and animal hides, have long since been dissolved by soil acids or devoured by soil bacteria. Archaeologists are left with a basic but minor portion of a people's material culture – tools made from durable and chemically inert stone – from which to piece together an ancient technology. The apparent simplicity of Stone Age technologies is largely a reflection of an inadequate archaeological record rather than of the simplicity of Stone Age peoples.

The record of past Arctic cultures is much more complete than that from most other regions of the world. Artifacts made from wood or bone, caribou antler or walrus ivory deteriorate very slowly after they are lost or discarded in an Arctic environment. During their first winter on the surface of an abandoned camp, the blast of dry winds and extreme cold for months on end brings about a process of natural freeze-drying, as efficient as any that can be produced by modern technology. Little chemical or biological deterioration can occur during the short, cool, and dry summers, and the freeze-drying process is repeated every winter as long as the artifact remains on the surface of the landscape. If the artifact becomes buried under wind-blown silt, or through the collapse of the turf-walled house in which it was lost, or beneath slowly growing vegetation and humus, it may become incorporated in permanently frozen soil. Permafrost acts as a gigantic deep-freeze, preserving for centuries artifacts as fragile as clothing made from animal skins sewn with sinew thread.

Another factor also assists archaeologists' interpretations of the

Palaeo-Eskimo way of life. The technology of the Palaeo-Eskimos and other Arctic peoples is particularly well suited to archaeological preservation and interpretation. Some cultural traditions, such as that of the Dene peoples of the northwestern Canadian forests, involve pride in being able to live with a minimum of material items. An axe, a knife, and a kettle are enough for ideal Dene to make a comfortable living from the forest they know so well. Even the knife can be replaced by a sharp flake knocked from a stone and discarded after use, and a temporary kettle can be quickly fashioned from birch bark. Home is a temporary brush shelter, food is provided by animals and fish snared or caught with lines made from roots or twisted bark, and comfort is a warm fire built on the bare earth. One makes a living by applying knowledge and skill rather than by using manufactured tools. Not surprisingly, the Dene leave little behind for archaeologists to interpret: a patch of ashes, a heap of decaying brush, and a scatter of animal bones that are soon dissolved by the acid soil beneath the spruce forest. Dene history is not very amenable to archaeological analysis, and indeed is very poorly known.

In contrast, the Palaeo-Eskimos needed manufactured tools in order to survive, and they made most of these tools from materials that preserve well in the dry gravel and frozen soils of the Arctic. Their environment provided no handy supplies of wood, spruce root, birch bark, or the other forest products from which more southerly peoples fashioned much of their material culture. Wood could be obtained only from scattered driftwood logs or from dangerous excursions to the edge of the Indian-occupied forests. Consequently, it was a valued commodity, carefully conserved and shaped to form artifacts for which no other material could be substituted, such as tent poles or the long shafts of spears and harpoons. Most of the artifacts elsewhere made from wood or bark the Palaeo-Eskimos made from animal products provided by their Arctic environment: bone, horn, antler, and ivory.

These relatively hard organic materials were difficult to work with and required a specialized technology of stone cutting tools. The manufacture of an ivory or antler tool demanded considerable skill and effort, and such artifacts were not simply made for immediate use and then discarded. Their manufacture was undertaken with care and with attention to style and design. As with all human technologies, concepts of style changed regularly and continuously throughout the 3,000 or more years that the Palaeo-Eskimos occupied the North American Arctic. The appropriate design for a tool or weapon was defined slightly differently by each generation of Palaeo-Eskimos, as it is in our own culture. And in the same way that we can tell from its style whether an automobile was made in the 1920s or 1940s or 1960s, archaeologists can date the artifacts found on a Palaeo-Eskimo site to a period of perhaps a century or two.

Most of the artifacts seen on Palaeo-Eskimo sites are so specialized that the archaeologist can reconstruct the activities carried out by the people who used them: hunting, butchering and skinning animals, sewing clothing, repairing weapons, and other daily tasks. With the animal bones that have accumulated as the by-products of meals eaten long ago, a picture of the economic life of an ancient community begins to take shape.

But the Palaeo-Eskimos did not limit their manufacturing skills to the production of economically useful tools and weapons. Unlike most other pre-industrial peoples, they transmuted many of their ideas about the spiritual world into material objects. Tiny carvings in ivory or wood portray spirit-animals, the faces of human-like beings, creatures suggesting human-animal transformations, as well as masks and other objects that appear to have been used in ritual activities. These 'fossilized ideas' allow archaeologists an unusual insight into the spiritual life of the first peoples of the Arctic.

Imagining History

The Palaeo-Eskimos provide a fascinating challenge to archaeology. The well-preserved tools, weapons, and carvings that they lost or abandoned in the snow and darkness of their winter camps remain as witnesses to a distant and very distinctive way of life. Yet these remains, abundant and pristine though they may be, are all that the archaeologist has to work with. The Palaeo-Eskimos left no cultural descendants to preserve the language, social arrangements, and belief systems that make up the greatest portion of any cultural tradition. There are no written records and only the vaguest of oral traditions resulting from other peoples' contact with Palaeo-Eskimos. As ingenious as the archaeologist can be in reconstructing the history and culture of these people on the basis of evidence dug from the frozen earth, the details of the final picture must be sketched from our general knowledge of Arctic peoples and the Arctic environment.

This process is not, of course, greatly different from any historical reconstruction. The reconstruction of Palaeo-Eskimo culture is simply an extreme case, and the resulting picture is somewhat more bizarre than the one usually produced by historians and archaeologists. In asserting the accuracy or plausibility of this picture, we can only claim that our picture fits what we know from the archaeological remains and what we know about the general nature of northern hunting cultures.

More intangible processes are also involved in the interpretations presented in the following pages. The reconstruction of Palaeo-Eskimo life demands more than simply objective analysis of artifacts and animal bones and the ruins of tent camps. The process also draws on an accumulation of thoughts that occur as one walks through an Arctic landscape essentially unchanged since it was first seen by human eyes 4,000 years ago; feelings that arise as one visits a thousand-year-old settlement whose owners appear to have abandoned it yesterday and who might be expected to return at any moment; and ideas that come from contemplating a tiny but powerful carving representing a magical creature from the mind of an ancient craftsman.

I have visited many Palaeo-Eskimo settlements. Although I have never met the people who lived there, I have often felt that they were close by. I have looked through their houses, walked and camped on their lands, enjoyed the serenity of their homesites, and marvelled at the work of their artists. And the more I learned, the more fascinating did this ancient and elusive people become.

CHAPTER 2

Eskimo History

When Europeans first penetrated the ice-filled seas protecting Arctic North America, they found the land occupied by a people remarkably different from any they had ever known. They were fascinated by the Eskimos' ability to survive comfortably in a land that Europeans found appallingly barren. The essential humanity of the Eskimos stood in conspicuous contrast to their way of life, which Europeans judged to be totally alien. John Ross wrote of his 1830 encounter with the Inuit of the eastern Arctic:

> It was for philosophers to interest themselves in speculating on a horde so small, and so secluded, occupying so apparently hopeless a country, so barren, so wild, and so repulsive; and yet enjoying the most perfect vigour, the most well-fed health, and all else that here constitutes, not merely wealth, but the opulence of luxury; since they were as amply furnished with provisions, as with every other thing that could be necessary to their wants.

European fascination with Eskimos soon led to conjectures about the origins of this remarkable Arctic people and of their extraordinary way of life. Early European theories viewed Eskimos as recent arrivals in the Arctic, having been forced into this bleak environment from a more civilized homeland in the Old World.

New World Tartars?

The mediaeval Norse occupants of Greenland may have been the first Europeans to note similarities between Eskimos and Old World peoples.

They called the Eskimos *skraelings,* a name possibly derived from 'Karelian' – the inhabitants of Karelia, in northern Finland and Russia – and that may have referred to the small dark-haired Saami people of Arctic Scandinavia. Christopher Hall, master of the ship *Gabriel* during Martin Frobisher's expedition to the Arctic in 1576, made a similar comparison when the English first met and traded with the Eskimos: 'They bee like to Tartars, with long black haire, broad faces, and flatte noses.'

Two centuries later, the first scholar to write on the subject of Eskimo origins based his conclusions on physical similarities between Eskimos and Asiatic peoples. David Crantz was a Moravian missionary; in 1767, he wrote a work called *History of Greenland,* in which he noted the differences between Eskimos and other aboriginal peoples of America and described resemblances between the Eskimos and the contemporaneous inhabitants of 'Great Tartary between Mongolia and the Arctic Ocean.' Crantz considered the historical upheavals that had seen repeated outbreaks of central Asiatic peoples into mediaeval Europe to have driven the Eskimos in the opposite direction, to find refuge on the bleak shores of Arctic North America.

Over the past century, it became apparent that the history of the Eskimos was considerably longer and more complex than envisioned by these early conjectures. The Eskimo language was not related to that of the Tartars, and their way of life could hardly have been more different. Speculations on Eskimo origins began to venture much deeper into the past.

Were the Eskimos Ice Age Europeans?

The second half of the nineteenth century produced a revolution in knowledge about the natural world, its history, and humanity's place in nature. The triumph of evolutionary theory opened the way to the development of several new branches of scientific investigation. Ethnologists began to prowl the outposts of colonial empires, noting and comparing the cultures, customs, and languages of diverse peoples. Anthropologists measured the head shape, skin colour, and other physical characteristics of the same groups. Archaeologists dug in the ruins of biblical cities, in the burial mounds of Europe and America, and in the caves and gravel deposits that yielded the first evidence of prehuman creatures. Geologists began to assemble pictures of Ice Age environments that were spectacularly different from those of the nineteenth-century world.

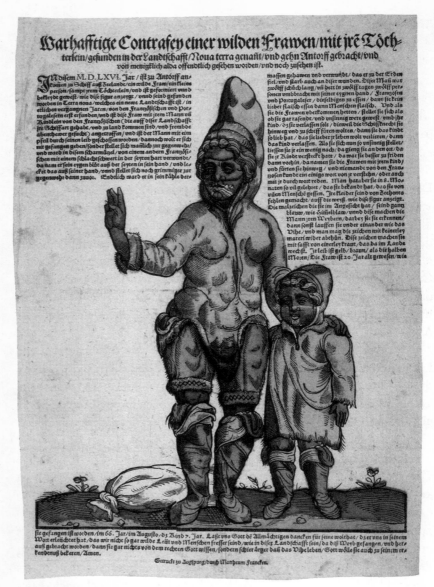

The first known European depiction of Inuit, from a handbill published in Augsburg in 1567. It shows a woman and child who had been kidnapped, probably from Labrador, and exhibited in Europe.

This sixteenth-century English engraving
representing Eskimo life in Arctic Canada
resulted from the experiences of those on
Martin Frobisher's voyage of 1576.

Harpoon heads, attached to a line and
designed to hook into the skin of a sea
mammal, were an essential invention in
allowing hunters to adapt to the Arctic
regions. This small ivory specimen is about
4,000 years old.

In this turmoil of intellectual activity, interest in the history of the Eskimos took a new turn. Renewed attention arose from the realization that, during the glacial periods described by geologists, environmental conditions in Europe had been very similar to those of Arctic North America. Ice Age Europe had been a treeless land roamed by vast herds of reindeer, which were in turn hunted by the Palaeolithic people whose remains were being unearthed from European caves by archaeologists. The reindeer of the Old World Arctic are closely related to New World caribou, one of the most important prey of many Eskimo groups.

Anthropologists pointed out that the skeletons of these ancient cave people were characterized by very long and narrow heads and were perfectly modern in form. Head shape was a feature of great interest to European scientists of the day. (We may remember that this period also saw the development of the so-called science of phrenology, which claimed to diagnose a person's intellectual and moral characteristics from the distribution of bumps on the skull.) The Eskimos of the eastern Arctic were also noted for their long, high skulls, and the similarity did not go unnoticed. Were Eskimos the descendants of ancient Europeans who had retreated northward with the shrinking Arctic environments at the end of the Ice Age and were eventually confined to the northern fringes of the New World?

To some prehistorians, the evidence was clear. Not only did long-headed Ice Age Europeans hunt arctic animals in a tundra landscape but the stone spearheads and bone harpoons recovered from their cave homes bore a general resemblance to those of traditional Eskimo manufacture. The Eskimos featured largely in the literature of Arctic exploration that flooded Europe during the late nineteenth century, and an ancient European homeland for the Eskimos was an attractive idea to Europeans, who were fascinated by this strange race.

Unfortunately for such a romantic notion, the developing techniques of twentieth-century archaeology soon indicated that there was no significant relationship between Ice Age Europeans and contemporary Eskimos. Improved dating techniques began to indicate that the long-headed reindeer-hunters of Ice Age Europe had occupied the continent between approximately 40,000 and 15,000 years ago, long before the first appearance of Eskimo culture. If a relationship between these ancient hunters and any New World population was to be suggested, it was more likely to be found with the earliest ancestors of the American Indians.

Evidence of ancestral Indian occupation of the western hemisphere could be traced to about the end of the last Ice Age, around the time that the early cave occupations of Europe came to an end. Perhaps the earliest reliable evidence of human occupation in the New World comes from a set of small caves near the northern edge of the forest in Canada's Yukon. Excavations in the Bluefish Caves, carried out by Jacques Cinq-Mars of the Canadian Museum of Civilization, yielded large quantities of animal bones from arctic species such as caribou and muskoxen, as well as from animals that became extinct at the end of the last Ice Age. Radiocarbon dating suggests that the Bluefish Cave occupation occurred at least as early as 15,000 years ago, and among the animal bones were a few chipped-stone tools similar to those used by European hunters of the same period. The ancestral Indians of the Bluefish Caves and the ancestral Europeans who hunted reindeer and painted the caves of France and Spain represent the extreme ends of a chain of similar, Arctic-adapted hunting peoples stretching across Eurasia during the last Ice Age.

Inland Origins?

While ancient links were emerging between the Stone Age hunters of Europe and the first American Indians, anthropologists and geographers had built a framework of speculation on Eskimo origins. By the beginning of the twentieth century, scholars had begun to place less emphasis on the physical traits of the Eskimo population and more on the development of their unique Arctic adaptation. This adaptation, it was soon realized, varied greatly from one group to the next. Some, such as the coastal Inuit of Labrador, southwestern Greenland, or northern Alaska, based most of their livelihood on hunting seals, walrus, and whales. Others, such as the Caribou Inuit living in the interior Barren Grounds region west of Hudson Bay, lived almost exclusively on caribou and freshwater fish. Still other groups mixed maritime and terrestrial hunting activities into ways of life that suited the environmental conditions of their local regions.

Historical speculation centred on the question of whether the Eskimos had originally been an inland people who had moved to the Arctic coast and learned to hunt sea mammals, or whether their ancestors had been maritime hunters of mammals and had adapted their economy to include the hunting of land animals and fish. Several early twentieth-

Beringia

Glaciated land at the
height of the Ice Age

MAP 2.1
Northern North America during the last Ice
Age. For much of the period between about
50,000 and 10,000 years ago, northern
Alaska and the adjacent Yukon were free
of ice and formed an eastern extension of
the Beringian plain joining Asia and
America.

∧ This small cave in a
limestone outcrop
above the northern
Yukon's Bluefish River
contains perhaps the
earliest clear evidence
of human occupation
in the New World. The
people who lived here
over 15,000 years ago
were probably ances-
tral American Indians.

> Arctic waters are
among the world's
richest in large sea
mammals. The Arctic
provided a plentiful
and dependable envi-
ronment for ancestral
Eskimo hunters, who
could capture animals
as large as whales,
such as this grey whale
feeding off a Bering
Sea beach.

century anthropologists saw the ancestral Eskimos as a people of the sub-Arctic interior, who had been pushed north to the Arctic coast and forced to adapt to this new and strange environment. The renowned scholar Franz Boas, writing in 1910, stated that 'the much-discussed theory of the Asiatic origin of the Eskimo must be entirely abandoned. [Investigations] … seem to show that the Eskimo must be considered as, comparatively speaking, new arrivals in Alaska, which they reached coming from the east.'

A more elaborate version of this scheme was conceived by Danish geographer H.P. Steensby. In 1916 Steensby published a treatise on Eskimo origins in which he postulated two 'layers' of Eskimo culture. The earlier layer he named Palaeo-Eskimo and described as an interior hunting culture similar to that of the Indians of the northern Canadian forests. At some time in the ancient past, these people had moved north to the Arctic coast, where they learned to hunt sea mammals. The resulting adaptation he termed Neo-Eskimo, the maritime way of life developed by Eskimos who had adapted to the conditions of northern coasts. Steensby's scheme of an older inland culture and more recent maritime culture set the stage for the first concentrated archaeological search for Eskimo origins.

Archaeological History

The archaeological investigation of Eskimo history began with the Danish Fifth Thule Expedition of 1921-4. The first four expeditions had taken place in Greenland and were devoted to other scientific studies. Led by Knud Rasmussen, a team of scholars in the Fifth Expedition crossed the Arctic from Greenland to Alaska, excavating archaeological sites and recording the cultural and physical traits of various Eskimo populations. Wherever they dug, the Danish archaeologists could trace Eskimo occupations to a very uniform culture, which appeared along the coasts of Greenland and Arctic Canada several centuries ago. They referred to this early way of life as the Thule culture because it had first been identified in old houses excavated near the settlement of Thule in northwestern Greenland.

The Thule way of life appeared to have been economically richer, more artistically sophisticated, and more uniform than were subsequent Inuit cultures of the past few centuries. Thule culture people were efficient hunters of sea mammals, including bowhead whales, the largest animals found in northern waters. Their ability to hunt such animals allowed them to settle in semi-permanent communities composed of houses built from

Bleached whale skulls protrude from an ancient Eskimo village on the Siberian coast of Bering Strait. Was this area the original homeland of the Eskimos?

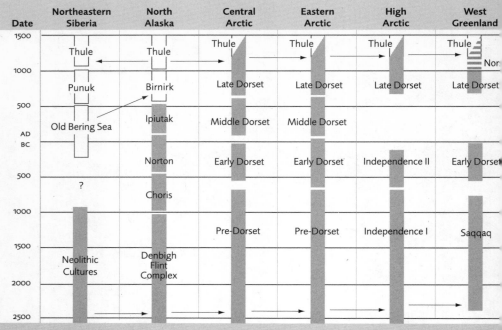

Date	Northeastern Siberia	North Alaska	Central Arctic	Eastern Arctic	High Arctic	West Greenland
1500	Thule	Thule	Thule	Thule	Thule	Thule
1000						Nor
	Punuk	Birnirk	Late Dorset	Late Dorset	Late Dorset	Late Dorset
500		Ipiutak	Middle Dorset	Middle Dorset		
AD BC	Old Bering Sea					
		Norton	Early Dorset	Early Dorset	Independence II	Early Dorset
500	?					
		Choris				
1000						
	Neolithic Cultures		Pre-Dorset	Pre-Dorset	Independence I	Saqqaq
1500						
		Denbigh Flint Complex				
2000						
2500						

FIGURE 2.1

The position in time and space of named archaeological cultures in Arctic North America

Key:

█ Palaeo-Eskimo Culture

☐ Neo-Eskimo (Inuit) Culture

≡ Greenlandic Norse

stone and turf, the roofs raftered with the huge jaw-bones of whales. This adaptation to maritime hunting was based on boats, weapons, and tools very similar to those of the Alaskan Eskimos who occupied the coasts of the Bering and Chukchi seas both before and during the Thule culture period.

Therkel Mathiassen, the leading archaeologist of the Fifth Thule Expedition, regarded the Thule culture people as the ancestors of the Canadian and Greenlandic Inuit. In contrast to Steensby's earlier theory, he suggested that ancestral Eskimos had been maritime hunters who had moved east from a homeland in coastal Alaska, and he dated this movement to approximately 1,000 years ago. Subsequent archaeological work has shown Mathiassen to have been essentially correct. Archaeology has also revealed a series of maritime-oriented cultures earlier than the Thule along the coasts of Alaska and eastern Siberia through which the ancestry of the Thule culture can be traced to between 2,000 and 3,000 years ago.

Thus, archaeology confirmed the much earlier speculations that Eskimos were relatively recent arrivals in Arctic Canada and Greenland and that their ancestors had come from Alaska. Nevertheless, all of the archaeological cultures that could be placed on the direct ancestral line of the Eskimos could be identified with Steensby's Neo-Eskimo culture, in which the basic economic pattern was grounded in maritime hunting of seals and whales. No archaeological trace could be found of the older, interior-oriented Palaeo-Eskimo culture that Steensby had postulated. Most archaeologists discarded the hypothetical Palaeo-Eskimos as the unnecessary constructs of an incorrect theory.

After centuries of speculation, archaeology finally showed that the origins of the Eskimo way of life derived not from that of the forest Indians of northern Canada, nor from that of 'Great Tartary between Mongolia and the Arctic Ocean,' nor from that of the Ice Age reindeer hunters of Europe. Rather, ancestral Eskimo culture was the most northern of a sequence of rich maritime economies that developed over the past few millennia along the coasts of the North Pacific Rim from Japan to British Columbia.

CHAPTER 3

An Asiatic People in America

The evidence that Therkel Mathiassen and his colleagues recovered on the Danish Fifth Thule Expedition of 1921-4 suggested that the Inuit, far from having an ancient history in the area, were descended from the whale-hunting Thule people who had expanded across Arctic Canada from Alaska within the past 1,000 years. The deeper roots of Eskimo history seemed to be found in the western Arctic, around the coasts of the Bering and Chukchi seas.

In 1924, as the Danish expedition was completing its traverse of Arctic America, a new and intriguing piece of the archaeological puzzle came to light. Diamond Jenness, an ethnologist with the National Museum of Canada in Ottawa, received a large collection of archaeological specimens. These had been excavated or purchased by Major L.T. Burwash, a government engineer working in the Arctic, from several locations around northern Hudson Bay. Many of the specimens were identical to those from the newly defined Thule culture and were similar in form to artifacts used by the traditional Inuit – those of the past century or so who lived a 'traditional' rather than a 'westernized' life. Other parts of the collection, however, were clearly different. Jenness described his approach to the collection:

> I placed on one side all the specimens that, from our own museum collections and from the works of Boas, Mathiassen, and others, I recognized as belonging to either the Thule or the modern culture. In other trays were laid all the fragments and pieces of doubtful use which had the same colour as the first lot and might reasonably be assigned to the same periods. There still remained some 500 specimens

so much darker than all the rest that a child could pick them out with certainty. The others were yellowish-brown; these were a deep chocolate. Their appearance strongly indicated that they were the oldest objects in the collection.

Jenness noted that the forms of these darkly patinated specimens were 'strange and unfamiliar,' unlike any known from the Thule culture or from traditional Inuit technology. Jenness concluded that these artifacts belonged to 'an old culture, hitherto unknown,' and he named it the Cape Dorset culture, after the location where a large portion of the collection had been excavated. For several decades the Cape Dorset culture remained an isolated enigma, the vestige of a way of life that might be older than that of the Inuit. It began attracting attention only after further excavations in Alaska and Greenland began to establish a context within which it could be understood.

The years following the Second World War saw a rapid increase in Arctic archaeology. Wartime advances in aircraft design and availability, as well as the growth of transportation facilities, made the Arctic more accessible to field workers. Archaeologists followed the engineers constructing the highways, airfields, and radar bases begun in wartime and expanded to meet the needs of the Cold War.

These were exciting times for archaeologists working in the Far North. The archaeology of the Arctic regions was practically unknown, yet it promised to yield answers to many questions dealing with relations between the cultures and peoples of the Old and New worlds. When did the first ancestors of the American Indians pass through the Arctic to reach North America? Were important elements of technology, such as ceramics or the bow and arrow, invented independently in the Old and New worlds, or did they spread across the Arctic regions between the two continents? Could archaeologists find traces of an ancient intercontinental tradition that could explain cultural similarities between the peoples of northern Canada, Siberia, and Europe? These were some of the issues raised at the time.

An Ancient Alaskan Culture

The summer of 1948 was particularly notable for Arctic archaeology. In Alaska, the American archaeologist Louis Giddings spent the summer excavating at Cape Denbigh on the coast of the Bering Sea. He had been

∧ The bow and finely tailored skin clothing were two Asiatic inventions probably brought to the New World by the Palaeo-Eskimos. This photograph of an Inuit hunter was taken in the central Arctic in 1915.

> Diamond Jenness, photographed as a member of the Canadian Arctic Expedition of 1913-18. A few years later he would define the Dorset culture on the basis of a collection of artifacts from the eastern Arctic.

Diamond Jenness defined the Dorset culture on the basis of this 1924 collection of artifacts from the eastern Arctic. The lighter coloured artifacts on the right were recognized as of Inuit styles; the darker coloured objects on the left were proposed to 'belong to an old culture, hitherto unknown.'

Small chipped-flint tools, made with great skill from highly coloured stones, are a hall-mark of the earliest people to occupy Arctic North America. They bear a resemblance to the tools used by Siberian Neolithic groups of the period around 5,000 years ago.

drawn to the location by the grass-covered house mounds of an old Eskimo village and found that the site had been heavily occupied by maritime hunting people ancestral to the Thule culture. The resulting layer of animal bones, stone tools, lamps, and other artifacts proved to be sixty centimetres thick and frozen, making its excavation a very slow process. Eventually, however, Giddings had the satisfaction of reaching the bottom and cutting into a clean sandy soil that seemed to have been the original surface on which the ancestral Eskimos had camped.

Far from marking the end of his summer's work, however, this day was to bring Giddings one of the most exciting finds of his career. Poking the tip of his trowel into the sandy loam that underlay the site, he felt it grate against something hard. A few more probes showed that there was a gritty layer about two centimetres below the surface of the sand. With the edge of his trowel he cut a small square, then slid the trowel beneath the block of soil and lifted it out. As Giddings describes it,

> The surface I saw could not have been more breathtaking had it been covered with gold. Glistening there with hardly a grain of fallen soil to mar them lay countless flakes of chert and obsidian and, unmistakably, the prismatic facets of microblades like those of the Middle Stone Age of Europe. Trembling with excitement at this rare disclosure, I continued to remove the sterile soil until I had exposed a glittering floor a yard across.

Louis Giddings recalls the excitement with which he returned from Cape Denbigh to his home at the University of Alaska to find two Danish archaeologists – Helge Larsen and Erik Holtved – visiting with new finds from a summer's work on the southern Bering Sea coast:

> We had talked over our prospects in the spring, and now, together once more with our scores of prize artifacts spread before us, we entered into a session as animated as that between mediaeval navigators who had discovered new continents ... In that single summer we had not only extended the knowledge of pre-Thule cultures for nearly the whole length of the Bering Sea region, but at Cape Denbigh had found a culture earlier than all the others – the Denbigh Flint complex – that recalled both the earliest archaeology of central Alaska and findings from the Gobi Desert of Asia. Our talk and excitement continued long into each night, and to nonarchaeological

visitors who dropped in briefly from time to time, our self-centered
and explosive conversation was like shaman talk in an unknown tongue.

The visiting Danish archaeologists had been tracing the remains of
the 2,000-year-old Ipiutak culture, named for a large site that Larsen had
excavated at Point Hope on the northwest coast of Alaska. They were
impressed by the Asiatic character of Ipiutak artifacts and art styles, which
resembled the art found in Bronze Age burial mounds of the southern
Siberian steppe, and even hinted at a distant relationship to Chinese art
styles. The Denbigh Flint Complex looked considerably older than
Ipiutak – possibly ancestral to it – and its chipped flint tools resembled
those used by Stone Age peoples of central Asia. Perhaps Giddings had
found evidence of an ancient link between Asia and America, a link
related to the origins of the Eskimos.

Helge Larsen recalled the Danish geographer Steensby's obsolete
concept of Palaeo-Eskimo and Neo-Eskimo cultural layers, and decided
that the term Palaeo-Eskimo effectively described the type of culture that
had been found at Ipiutak and at Cape Denbigh. Unlike Steensby, however, who saw the Palaeo-Eskimos as a people of the northern Canadian
forests, Larsen suggested that they were an ancient reindeer-hunting people of interior Siberia, who had followed migrating reindeer north to the
Arctic coast. Here they had learned to hunt seals and walrus and had
spread eastward across Bering Strait to become the first inhabitants of the
New World Arctic.

A Discovery in Independence Fiord

While Giddings was uncovering the hidden living floor and tiny glitter-
ing stone tools left by a previously unknown people on the west coast of
Alaska, the Danish explorer Eigil Knuth was walking over a newly discovered archaeological site in Pearyland, the barren and uninhabited
country extending north from the Greenland ice cap to the Arctic Ocean.
The site at Deltaterrasserne was discovered in September of 1948, during
the second summer of a multi-year research expedition to Pearyland.
Knuth, who organized and led the Danish Pearyland Expedition, wrote:

> Luckily, the settlement on the Deltaterrasserne was on the whole better
> preserved than the others in the fiord. The stone constructions on
> [terraces] at levels ranging from 5 to 23 m above the sea, had been
> erected from [such] big stones that they were observed from a boat

on the water ... In spite of the barrenness of the terrain the place possessed a romantic beauty, intensified by the devotion invariably felt
by walking around in a prehistoric town so far beyond the limits of
history and reason.

Knuth had not expected to find such impressive evidence of
human occupation in this barren land, where small herds of muskoxen
provided the only prey for hunters. He was even more surprised by the
unique form of the boulder structures and chipped-flint artifacts scattered
about them, which were very different from those of known Inuit cultures.
He realized that he had found the remains of a pre-Inuit occupation of
this most remote and bleakest region of Arctic North America.

Knuth named his find the Independence culture, after Independence Fiord, the central geographical feature of Pearyland. Like his com-
patriot Larsen, Eigil Knuth was reminded of Steensby's Palaeo-Eskimos.
Not only did the remains of dwellings found at Deltaterrasserne resemble
the ones Steensby had conjectured for the Palaeo-Eskimos but the bones
of muskoxen and fish found in the adjacent refuse heaps confirmed that
the Independence people, like the hypothetical Palaeo-Eskimos, had focused
their livelihood on the resources of the land and inland waters of Greenland's interior. Knuth began to think of Pearyland as the final link in
Steensby's 'Muskox Way,' the route followed by early Palaeo-Eskimo land
mammal hunters from the coniferous forests to the farthest reaches of the
Arctic. Indeed, he was excited to find an old conjectural 'path' existing in
present reality when he wandered up the broad valley joining one of the
heads of Independence Fiord with that of the next large fiord complex to
the west:

> And when I went exploring the river from the Midsummer Lakes in
> the great diagonal valley my route took me to an old, trodden ani-
> mal trail that over a distance of 15 miles connected the fiord with
> the lakes. It was a visible, vivid part of Steensby's postulated 'musk
> oxen route,' the migration roads of the Palaeo-Eskimos from Arctic
> Canada to Northeast Greenland, registered on Steensby's map from
> 1916, with a short cut to the west of the Pearyland peninsula
> through that very same valley.

The discoveries of 1948 opened new vistas to the archaeology of
Arctic North America. The archaeological conferences of the early 1950s
heard rumours of the two ancient finds that had been made at opposite

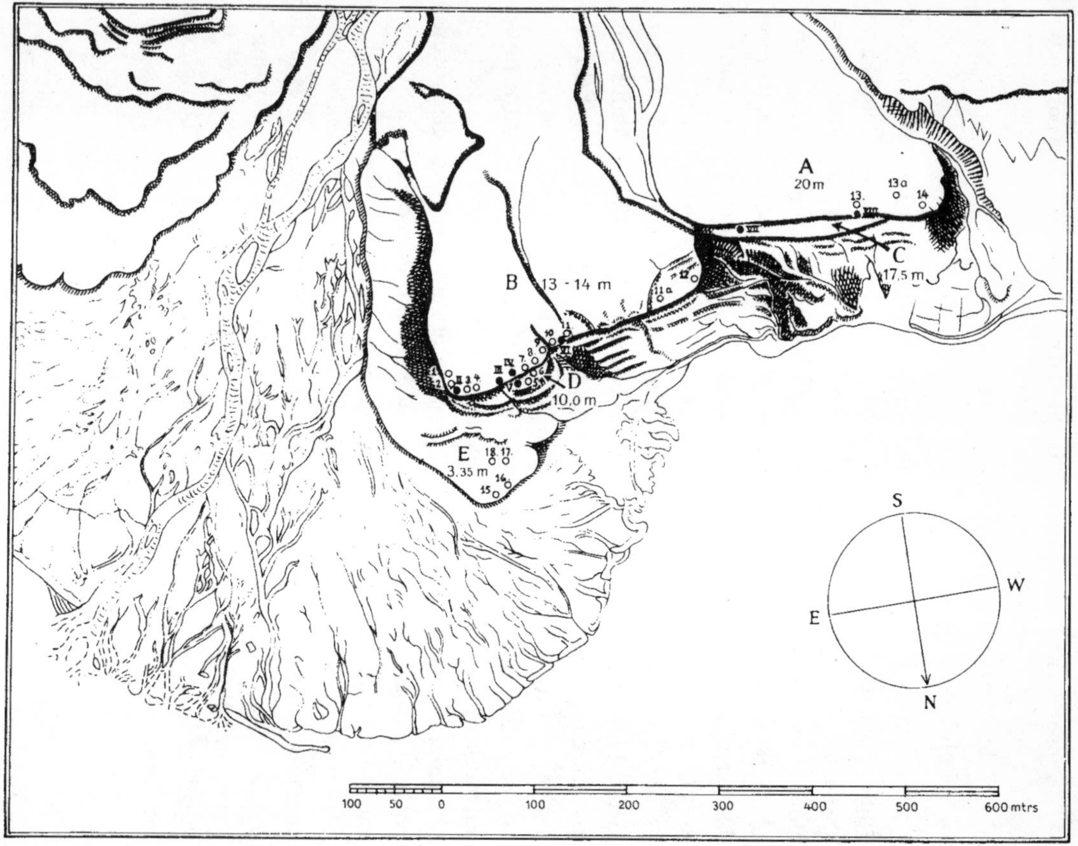

MAP 3.1
Eigil Knuth's plan of an ancient settlement, which he discovered at Deltaterrasserne, on the shores of Independence Fiord. Letters A to E refer to occupied terrace levels, measured in metres above sea level.

Source: Eigil Knuth, *Reports from the Musk-ox Way* (Copenhagen: privately published 1984)

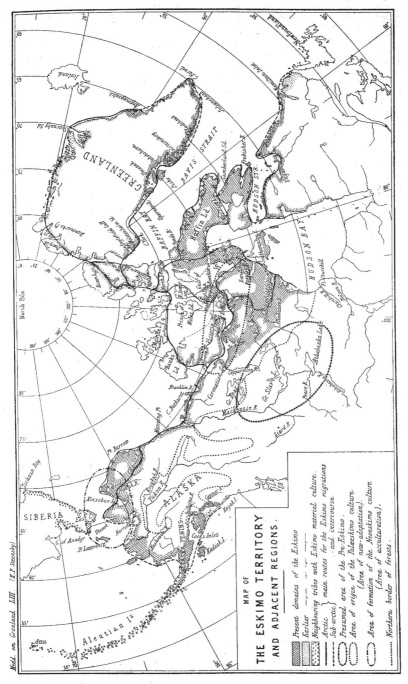

MAP 3.2

Eskimo origins according to H.P. Steensby, 1916. The most northerly black
line, through the Arctic islands and around northern Greenland, marks
the hypothetical Muskox Way.

Source: H.P. Steensby, *An Anthropogeographical Study of the Origins of the Eskimo
Culture,* Meddelelser om Grønland 53 (Copenhagen: Commission for Scientific
Research in Greenland 1916).

ends of Arctic North America. As descriptions and photographs of the artifacts began to circulate, it became apparent that the tiny chipped-stone tools of the Denbigh Flint Complex and those of the Independence culture were very similar. Both sets of artifacts had obviously been made and lost by the same ancient people who had once occupied the entire Arctic from Alaska to Greenland. A new depth had suddenly been added to Arctic history, and a new population – the Palaeo-Eskimos – to the cast of New World peoples.

The history of the New World could no longer be simply divided between Indians and Eskimos. The first occupants of the Arctic had turned out to be neither, but a mysterious third group whose cultural roots appeared to extend into the distant forests of Siberia.

Siberian Similarities

Both Louis Giddings on the shores of Bering Strait and Eigil Knuth in far northern Greenland saw an Old World ancestry in the archaeological materials they had discovered. Most immediately noticeable were the microblades that made up a large proportion of the artifacts in both collections. These were narrow slivers of glass-like flint, with long straight edges as sharp as razor blades. They were made by a very specialized technique, which allowed a flint worker to produce large numbers of very similar and regularly shaped tools quickly. These microblades could then be set into the edges of wooden or bone handles to form extremely sharp-edged knives, spearheads, sickles, or swords. The microblade technique was developed in Eurasia around the end of the last Ice Age, and these very efficient stone cutting edges were used by the later Stone Age and early Bronze Age peoples from Europe to Japan. The discovery of a microblade-using culture across Arctic North America suggested the intrusion of a Eurasian technology, if not a Eurasian people, into the New World.

An Old World derivation was also suggested for another type of stone tool that was conspicuous in these collections. Burins were the primary tools used in cutting bone, antler, or ivory in order to fashion these materials into artifacts. These small, plane-like instruments, with cutting edges only a couple of millimetres wide, were again made and sharpened by a technique that had been developed in the Old World Stone Age. The microblades, burins, and tiny burin spalls formed in sharpening the latter tools linked this ancient Arctic technology firmly to Eurasia rather than

A tiny hearth on an Arctic beach is
evidence of occupation by an ancient
pre-Eskimo population.

Sharp-edged microblades, chipped in
series from cores like this one – the largest
object in the photograph – were another
link between Asia and the first occupants
of Arctic North America.

to North America. The small chipped-stone weapon points, scrapers, and other implements found in these early Arctic sites showed a general resemblance to tools excavated from settlements in the region of Lake Baikal, and similar collections were known from elsewhere in central and eastern Siberia. Archaeologists began to talk of an Arctic Small Tool tradition, choosing a name that reflected the tiny size of most Palaeo-Eskimo tools, and thinking of it as a tool-making tradition rooted in the Neolithic cultures of Asia.

The first discoveries of Palaeo-Eskimo sites coincided with the invention of the radiocarbon dating technique. The new technique allowed archaeologists to detect the age of an ancient site by analyzing small samples of charcoal or other common materials, and produced a revolution in knowledge of prehistory. Samples of charcoal from Palaeo-Eskimo sites were among the first to be dated by the new technique; the results indicated an age of between 3,000 and 4,000 years ago, far earlier than anyone had suspected for an occupation of Arctic North America. These dates, however, agreed with the age estimates for the Siberian Neolithic collections with which Palaeo-Eskimo artifacts were compared.

Even more striking than the similarity of stone tools was the resemblance between the dwellings that Knuth discovered at Deltaterrasserne and traditional forms known from northern Eurasia. The ancient muskox hunters of far northern Greenland had lived in tents, almost certainly covered with muskox hides over a framework of driftwood poles. The archaeological remains of these structures were marked by an oval ring of boulders, used to hold down the edges of the tent, centred on a box-shaped hearth built of stone slabs set on edge in the gravel. Flanking the central hearth were two parallel rows of vertically set stone slabs, running from front to back of the dwelling and forming a midpassage forty to eighty centimetres wide. The dwelling was thus divided into three areas: a living area on either side of the central feature, and the midpassage itself, which in turn was divided by the central hearth. This very distinctive structural arrangement of a dwelling – the function of which is not known – is also found in northern Eurasia, where it was characteristic of the traditional house used by the Saami people.

There were other hints that these newly discovered people, who made stone tools using techniques invented in Eurasia and who lived in tents arranged in a northern Eurasian style, used other elements of Old

∧ A ring of stones on a
   High Arctic beach marks
   the site of an early
   Palaeo-Eskimo camp.
   The 'passage' formed by
   lines of upright stones
   and the central square
   box hearth were a striking characteristic of the
   early sites discovered in
   Independence Fiord.
   The ice axe in the foreground is one metre
   long.

> This eighteenth-century
   drawing of a Saami (Lapp)
   dwelling from northern
   Scandinavia shows the
   same distinctive passage
   and hearth arrangement
   seen in the remains of
   early Palaeo-Eskimo
   structures.

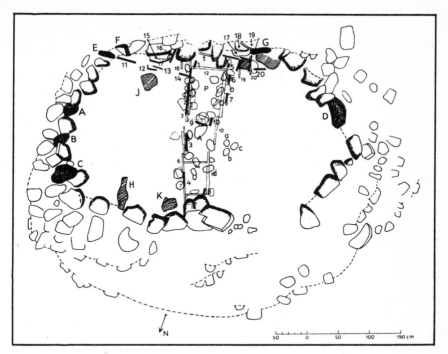

FIGURE 3.1
Eigil Knuth's drawing of one of the early
Palaeo-Eskimo dwellings that he excavated
in Independence Fiord. Letters and
numbers refer to various features of the
structure.

Source: Eigil Knuth, *Reports from the Musk-ox Way*
(Copenhagen: privately published 1984)

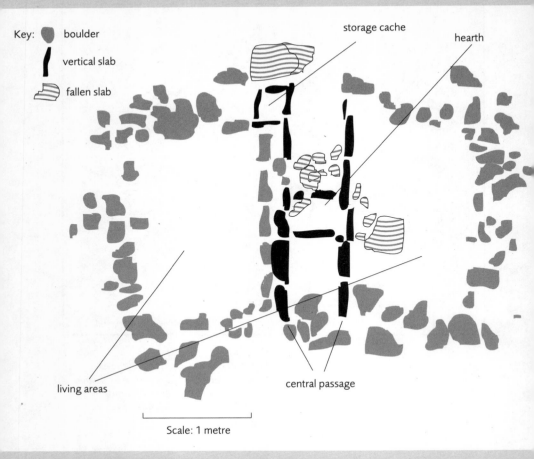

Key:

- boulder
- vertical slab
- fallen slab

storage cache

hearth

living areas

central passage

Scale: 1 metre

FIGURE 3.2
Plan drawing of the Independence
dwelling shown at the top of page 38

World technology to help them adapt to Arctic conditions. Tiny chipped-stone weapon points, recovered from the gravel floors of their tents, could only have been used effectively to tip arrows; the bow was invented in the Old World at some time after the end of the last Ice Age, and was not known in North America until relatively recently. Although no clothing is preserved from early Palaeo-Eskimo sites, it also seems likely that finely tailored skin clothing, cut to patterns developed in the Arctic regions of Siberia, was an important part of Palaeo-Eskimo adaptation. Fragments of broken bone needles are among the most common artifacts recovered from Palaeo-Eskimo dwelling sites, and are our only witness to the labour and artistry of those who stitched the garments that enabled humans to first occupy Arctic North America.

Superb skin clothing, the bow and arrow, efficient techniques for transforming stones into razor-sharp cutting tools, and a dwelling that combined portability with protection and comfort were the major items of technology that the Palaeo-Eskimos brought to the New World. As well, they must have carried not only an excellent knowledge of the Arctic environment and its animals, and of their own history and society, but also a distinctive view of the world and the place of humans in it. In their successful occupation of Arctic North America, these traditions, beliefs, and ideas were at least as important as the technologies that left hard archaeological remains.

Who Were the Palaeo-Eskimos?

Among the puzzles not yet answered by the archaeological evidence is the relationship of these first explorers of the Arctic to peoples of the present world. Considering the Siberian affinities of their technology, they were probably not related to North American Indians. The few skeletons found in burials that can probably be identified as Palaeo-Eskimo are of a physical type shared by Eskimos and the peoples of far northeastern Siberia. Despite the name 'Palaeo-Eskimos,' given them by archaeologists, their relationship to Eskimo or Inuit peoples is not at all clear. They were more probably related to the ancestors of the Eskimo-like peoples who occupy northeastern Siberia today, the Chukchi. Whoever they were, and whatever language they spoke, the archaeological traces of the Palaeo-Eskimos suggest intellectual and artistic accomplishments that compel both admiration and fascination.

Chukchi hunters of northeastern Siberia.
Their ancestors were probably closely
related to the Palaeo-Eskimos of Arctic
North America.

A Chukchi family and their dwelling, as drawn by an early nineteenth-century artist.

CHAPTER 4

The People of the Muskox Way

The northern margin of the American mainland slips gradually beneath the sea along an irregular and unfinished coast. Under the shallow water, a continental shelf extends 2,000 kilometres north toward the Pole, outcropping in hundreds of islands that form one of the world's great archipelagos, over one million square kilometres. For most of the year, these islands are locked together by sea ice, the frozen water merging with snow-covered land into a single bleak terrain. Even during the short summer period of open water, most of the islands are separated by narrow, ice-choked straits only a few kilometres in width.

The most conspicuous boundary within the Arctic Archipelago is Parry Channel, a major passage that joins Baffin Bay in the east with the Arctic Ocean in the west. The various bodies of water that make up this channel – Lancaster Sound, Barrow Strait, Viscount Melville Sound, and M'Clure Strait – are over fifty kilometres wide at their narrowest point and run approximately along the seventy-fifth parallel. Parry Channel serves as a convenient marker separating the Low Arctic islands, which more closely resemble the continental mainland, from the region known as the High Arctic.

The High Arctic

The High Arctic is a land of gravel, rock, and ice. Along its western rim, low grey islands barely emerge from the surrounding ice, their western coasts ground continuously by the massive floes of the polar pack. In contrast, the eastern islands contain the highest North American mountains east of the Rockies; many are capped by enormous ice fields, and glaciers flow down valleys to launch icebergs into the surrounding seas. The adjacent portion of northern Greenland, isolated from more southerly regions by the Inland Ice and separated from the islands of Arctic Canada only by a narrow and frozen strait, is an integral part of the High Arctic zone.

The defining characteristics of the Arctic are found at their most extreme in the regions north of Parry Channel. At the Arctic Circle the midnight sun appears on only one day at midsummer, but in the High Arctic the sun remains continually above the horizon for between two and four months each year. The midwinter night lasts for an equivalent length of time, with the coldest months of the year illuminated only by twilight, the aurora, and the circling moon. The warmest month is only a few degrees above freezing, the coldest have an average temperature below minus thirty degrees Celsius, and snow can fall at any time of the year. The climate is classified as Polar Desert, providing so little warmth and moisture that vegetation mantles the surface only in favoured locations. Even in areas where local climate and soil conditions encourage a continuous cover of tundra plants, these rarely reach above ankle height. In many areas, each tiny individual herb or dwarf willow shrub is separated from the next by metres of gravelly soil or broken rock.

Despite the apparent meagreness of the High Arctic tundra, it supports a surprising number of grazing animals. Bands of Peary caribou, tiny animals with coats as pale as snow-veiled tundra, drift across the landscape like ungainly ghosts. Families of muskoxen, their horns gleaming and tattered, windblown coats hanging to the ground, resemble the last survivors of the Pleistocene Age as they lumber on their mysterious journeys. Huge white hares hop from flower to flower or cluster in groups so dense that entire hillsides appear to be alive. During the brief summer months, the edges of tundra ponds are alive with broods of snow geese, brant, and eider ducks.

Although migratory birds abandon the area by September, the mammals are year-round occupants. The light winter snowfall and the constant winds that sweep the landscape clear of snow allow grazing animals continuous access to their food supply. Throughout the darkness of the long midwinter night, muskoxen and caribou and hare continue to wander about the countryside, feeding and providing in their turn a food resource for predatory wolves and scavenging foxes. At some time

∧ Large white hares are a feature of many
High Arctic landscapes.

∨ Peary caribou drift across the bleakest
islands of the High Arctic.

between 5,000 and 4,000 years ago, a new and more deadly predator arrived in the High Arctic.

High Arctic Archaeology

The Arctic is kind to archaeologists, as was pointed out in an earlier chapter. In a region where preservation is generally good, the High Arctic is particularly generous. The extremely cold and dry conditions that prevail along the northern rim of the Arctic preserve objects as small and fragile as a bone sewing needle that was lost over 4,000 years ago. The absence of disturbance and soil development makes it possible to find such a needle four millennia later.

In most areas, surface vegetation is so sparse that it helps the archaeologist find an ancient camping place rather than hiding its meagre remains. The diminutive tundra plants of the High Arctic flourish only where nutrients and moisture are available, and a primary source of such nutrients is found in the animal bones and other refuse left around an old camp. An isolated patch of flowers in a landscape of barren gravel, visible from a kilometre or more away, provides an excellent marker for the spot where a family camped for a few days several millennia in the past. The remains of such small-scale occupations can be easily identified in the High Arctic, although they would be totally invisible in the more heavily vegetated regions to the south.

These conditions of preservation and visibility help to explain why the High Arctic has produced a disproportionate amount of information on the early phases of Palaeo-Eskimo culture. At a time when knowledge of the Palaeo-Eskimos in the western Arctic was limited to the stone tools found at Cape Denbigh and a few similar small collections that were generally found by accident, Eigil Knuth was tracing entire settlements along the shores of northern Greenland's Independence Fiord. His interpretations of the Independence culture and reconstruction of the way of life that it represented gave archaeologists their first relatively complete picture of a Palaeo-Eskimo society and its economy. This depiction became basic to archaeological thinking about the Palaeo-Eskimos. It therefore seems appropriate to begin our examination of Palaeo-Eskimo history in the High Arctic with a description of their most northerly and most distinctive adaptation. In the following chapter we will return to more southerly Arctic regions in order to follow the Palaeo-Eskimos from

Siberia across Arctic North America and eventually to the extreme regions of the High Arctic.

The People of the Muskox Way

When Eigil Knuth led the Danish Pearyland Expedition to the far northern coast of Greenland, he hoped to trace the route by which the Inuit reached an eastern Greenland homeland. Exploring the bare gravel beaches of Independence Fiord, he discovered no remains of the heavy boulder-and-turf winter houses which are the most visible archaeological mark of traditional Inuit occupation. He found only tent rings, circles or ovals of boulders that once weighted the skirts of portable, skin-covered dwellings.

Although the existence of tent rings proved that humans had once occupied the extreme High Arctic, far north of areas inhabited by the Inuit of the past few centuries, Knuth had been advised by more experienced archaeologists that very little could be learned from excavating them. He was told that tent camps, which were temporary occupation sites used for only a few days at a time, lacked the archaeological evidence that accumulates as refuse around a dwelling occupied for an entire winter. Tents were also occupied during the summer season, the sunlit and snow-free portion of the year, when artifacts were more rarely lost than in dark and snowy winter camps. Indeed, this is generally good advice for archaeologists investigating Inuit occupations of the past few centuries. The sites of Inuit tent rings are notoriously barren of artifacts and stand in remarkable contrast to the artifact-rich remains of winter house occupations.

Knuth, however, had no alternative but to investigate the tent rings scattered along the coasts of Independence Fiord, and the few artifacts that he recovered from them were quite different from the Inuit hunting weapons and household utensils he had expected to find: 'But when the aircraft had left us to our fate in Peary Land there *were* no winter houses, only tent rings, and it was necessary to dig in them. A large number gave no find, but when at last remains were found they were quite small things of *flint* of ... Stone Age types.'

As we have seen, these tiny chipped-flint tools – razor-edged microblades, burins for working antler or ivory, scrapers for preparing skin clothing, and sharp points for weapons – were indeed 'of Stone Age types.' They showed no resemblance to the tools of the traditional Inuit, who for at least the past millennium had replaced chipped-stone artifacts

An archaeologist wanders among traces of
Independence I occupation on northern
Ellesmere Island.

with cutting tools of metal or ground slate. They related to a distinctly older technology, not previously encountered in the New World Arctic.

The tent rings themselves were also quite different from the simple circles of boulders that mark the temporary summer camps of Inuit hunters: 'Many of the tent rings possessed a remarkably solid and house-like construction, [with] a central corridor of sunken stone slabs placed edgeways, yet all so low that they presupposed a skin tent as roof. In the centre of the middle of the corridors there were open hearths with thick layers of charcoal and burnt bones. Most of these, plus the unburnt bones in the midden sites, derived from musk-oxen.'

This very distinctive form of tent foundation again pointed to an ancient and non-Inuit style of dwelling. Moreover, it suggested that many of these tiny archaeological sites were not the remains of simple, temporary tent camps. The builders of these structures had apparently invested the type of effort that we would expect only from people who anticipated using the dwelling for a considerable length of time. Knuth began to wonder if this discovery was related to the lack of evidence for winter houses in the area. Was it possible that the first occupants of the High Arctic had not passed the winters in heavily built houses insulated with turf or snow but had lived in tents throughout the entire year?

The unlikely suggestion that the Independence people made year-round use of tent dwellings was supported by other evidence recovered from their camps. All tundra cultures known previously to archaeologists had heated and lighted their winter houses with pottery or soapstone lamps, burning oil derived from the fat of seals or other sea mammals. Yet the camps of the Independence people produced no traces of oil lamps. Even if this lack of evidence could be ascribed to poor archaeological luck, it was difficult to imagine where the Independence people could have obtained oil to burn for winter light and warmth. The ice-choked waters of Independence Fiord, like many High Arctic channels, support very small seal populations, and none of the larger sea mammals frequent the area. No sea mammal bones were found in the middens associated with Independence structures. Instead, the middens were full of the bones of muskoxen, and these large ungulates were obviously the most important prey of the Independence people. Muskoxen are a good source of meat but not of fat or oil, and muskox hunters could not have accumulated enough tallow to heat and light their winter dwellings with oil-burning lamps.

Herds of muskoxen provide the most dependable year-round resource for hunting peoples in the High Arctic.

Mapping the remains of an Independence I
tent in the High Arctic.

The dwellings of the Independence people probably resembled this skin tent used by the Copper Inuit of the central Arctic during the early twentieth century. Note the ball of willow twigs gathered for fuel.

The only alternative to an oil lamp available to High Arctic hunters would have been an open fire, and box-shaped hearths lined with stone slabs were a central feature of Independence structures. Even the most elaborately constructed dwellings, which appeared to have been built for lengthy occupation during the winter months, had a central hearth filled with charcoal and burned bone fragments. But a smoky, open fire cannot be used in the tightly closed and insulated houses traditionally used by the Inuit and other tundra peoples, built from boulders, turf, wood, or snow. The need for a smoke vent negates the heat-holding advantages of such a structure. If the Independence people used open fires for winter heat and light, then they probably lived in tents throughout the year. The implications of such a possibility, in a treeless land where fuel must be gathered with immense labour and winter darkness and intense cold are unbroken for months on end, are rather appalling.

A Polar Way of Life

When we try to envision the manner in which the Independence people lived, our first response might be to base our reconstruction on the way of life followed by the traditional Inuit of the past few centuries in the eastern Arctic. But this approach encounters immediate problems. For one thing, no traditional Inuit groups lived this far north, and none had been forced to accommodate their lives to a winter night that lasted for several months of the year. Secondly, the Inuit were primarily a coastal people; their adaptation to the Arctic environment was based on the hunting of sea mammals, which in turn allowed them to shelter from the winter in insulated and lamp-warmed houses. Finally, in the event of local hunting failures, Inuit dogsleds and boats gave them a degree of mobility and security that must have been unknown to the Independence people.

Inuit life provides a poor model for that of the first humans to occupy the High Arctic. In reconstructing the lives of the Independence people, we must rely almost entirely on what we can deduce from the scattered remains of their camps, the refuse and the lost artifacts that they left behind. Beyond this we are in the realm of the imagination, informed only by what we know of the ways of life common to all non-agricultural peoples, and especially to those living in Arctic environments. The most plausible picture would look something like the following.

Muskoxen were the basic and central focus of life for the Independence people of the extreme High Arctic. Herds of the huge shaggy beasts grazed every valley when the first hunters explored the country. They showed no apprehension of the two-legged newcomers and were easy prey to stone-tipped arrows and thrown lances. Even when they learned to run from human hunters, the hunters' dogs could soon bring them to a stop. A dog triggers the muskoxen's instinctive defence against wolves, forming a defensive line or circle and holding it until the canine enemy is wounded or loses interest in the attack. This is effective against dogs but leaves the muskoxen vulnerable to the dog's human companions, who can slaughter the stationary animals at will.

For people who know muskox behaviour and who learn the local geography, obtaining food becomes a routine business. The Independence hunters would scan areas where the animals were known to graze, select a likely herd and walk to the locality where they were feeding or resting, set their dogs on the herd and close in with bows and lances. When the remainder of the herd finally broke in panic or despair, the skinning and butchering of the dead animals would begin. Some of the meat was cached on rock or dry gravel, covered with a pile of heavy boulders to deter foxes and wolves. Portions of the meat, along with the hides and horns, were packed into bundles and carried back to the camp. This was the most difficult part of the operation; the women of the camp, if they were not a part of the original hunting party, were probably recruited to share in the heavy labour.

Unlike most other Arctic animals, muskoxen are not migratory and are available to hunters in both summer and winter. Whereas a typical Inuit group of the past century might hunt whales and walrus in the open water of summer, caribou during the fall migration, and seals at their winter breathing holes, the Independence people could follow a single pattern of hunting and living throughout the year. Midwinter hunts were simply colder, darker, and probably more distant, as the muskoxen had abandoned the valleys for upland areas where winds swept the snow from the vegetation on which they grazed throughout the long winter night. Summer hunts, in contrast, must have been much more comfortable and productive. The summer diet could be varied with ducks or geese, the eggs of nesting birds, unwary young hares, and the occasional seal surprised as it idled along a narrow lead in the ice. Arctic char, probably speared during their annual migrations to the sea through the shallow rivers of the

Muskoxen are vulnerable to human hunters accompanied by dogs. Almost an entire herd might be killed before breaking from its defensive formation.

High Arctic, must have provided a welcome food source in the few streams large enough to support sizable fish populations. Caribou would have been hunted throughout the year, but the hunt was probably intensified in late summer and early autumn, when the animals' hides were in prime condition for use as clothing.

With plentiful food, life must have been joyful in the summer camps of the Independence people. For four months the sun never set, affording a freedom unknown to non-Arctic peoples. The weather was pleasantly warm (usually ranging between zero and ten degrees Celsius), the sun usually shone, yet there were few days hot enough to inflict the hordes of mosquitoes that are the scourge of more southerly regions of the Arctic.

Judging from the size of most archaeological sites, Independence camps were generally small, perhaps ranging between one and five tents sheltering a number of small, related families. Camp size would vary depending on the season, the number of muskoxen in the local area, and the particular endeavours in which each family was engaged. In addition to the daily tasks of hunting and preparing food, summer must have been a time for replenishing supplies and preparing equipment. A trip of a few days' duration might be required in order to gather flint from an isolated quarry. Another expedition might be mounted in order to search stretches of coast where driftwood logs were known to accumulate. Some groups, whose traditional territory contained sources of flint or wood, might gather a surplus and trade with neighbouring groups in return for other materials, food supplies, dogs, or finished artifacts.

Trading trips might be timed to coincide with a run of char in a certain river, the egg-laying season at a certain nesting cliff, or other resource concentrations that would attract several small groups to a brief gathering. Such gatherings must have been of immense social importance to people who spent most of the year in small and isolated bands. They were opportunities for marrying, renewing friendships, showing off new children, commiserating over deaths and misfortunes, and learning the news about events and conditions in other parts of the country. There must have been dances, songs, and stories that lasted all night before each small band set off in a different direction for another season of isolation. Most important for social harmony, they provided an opportunity for individuals and families to leave a group in which they were having troubles and to try their luck with another band of relatives.

Most of the summer season must have been spent in more tedious occupations. Each camp was a tiny island of humanity in a vast and silent landscape: a few tents, a couple of dogs tied to boulders, perhaps the smoke of a small cooking fire, children playing and women working on the dry gravel near the tents. As in most non-agricultural societies, women's work was probably as strenuous as and much more unrelenting than that of the men. Cooking a meal involved a lengthy hunt for fuel: collecting small chunks of dry moss or lumps of muskox dung, the arm-wrenching labour of pulling heather and dwarf willow stems from frozen ground or sticks of driftwood from frozen beaches, or smashing animal bones from earlier meals. The tiny flame struck from flint and pyrites had to be carefully nursed and shielded from the wind and the meat cut into pieces small enough to be broiled or to fit into a skin bucket to be boiled with hot stones. Given the amount of labour involved, it would not be surprising to find that much of the food was eaten raw.

Much of the chore of moving camp probably also fell to the women. These movements most likely occurred at intervals of a few days throughout the summer as the muskoxen moved away from a hunted area, as other food resources became available, or in order to process a major kill more efficiently. The entire family may have helped to dismantle the tents and pack the belongings, but much of the carrying probably fell to the women and girls, while the men scouted and hunted along the route. The construction of a new stone hearth and midpassage may also have been a task for the women, whose labour was centred on this important part of the dwelling.

The most unremitting summer task faced by women, however, was the preparation of skins, sewing of new clothes, and repair of old. Caribou skins used for clothing, muskox hides for blankets and tent covers, and perhaps sealskins for waterproof boots had to be scraped clean of fat and tissue, soaked, dried, scraped, kneaded, and scraped again to make them supple enough to work. Sinew had to be stripped from the tendons of caribou and muskoxen and separated to form strong thread. Traditional patterns and techniques of measuring were learned from childhood, but cutting clothing still demanded skill and great care. Sewing was done with small needles, carved and polished from bone and with tiny drilled eyes, as delicate and much more fragile than the steel needles used by modern needleworkers. The fragility of the needles, as well as the perseverance of Independence women, is evidenced in the large numbers of needle fragments found in the gravel floors of their ancient tents. They attest to the importance of women's skills and fortitude as the essential element that allowed the Independence people to forge a way of life in the High Arctic.

As in all northern traditional societies, while women worked in skins, the skills and strengths of the men were probably focused on the manufacture and repair of tools and weapons from hard materials. Stone, bone, ivory, antler, horn, and wood all had an important place in the Independence people's technology. Whenever hunting was prohibited by fog, snow, or the unavailability of animals in the region, men could find weapons to repair, knives or scrapers to sharpen, and needles to carve.

The most esoteric skill known to Independence men was the chipping of flint to make sharp-edged cutting tools and pointed weapons. Flint working is one of humankind's oldest arts and one of the most difficult to master. The early Palaeo-Eskimos were expert in the craft, producing tiny artifacts with a form and symmetry surpassing that of most stone-working cultures. The quality of workmanship is so high among the lost and broken tools found in their camps that some of the work was probably done by specialists whose skill and expertise was widely recognized in the community.

Less skilled but also demanding of time and energy was the manufacture of objects from organic materials. The scarcest of these materials was wood, which was obtained solely from the driftwood logs scattered along High Arctic beaches. When a large spruce log from a distant Siberian river was found, it would be split and carved to form tent poles, bows, harpoon shafts, and other necessary objects. Like other Arctic peoples, the Independence craftsmen used animal-based substitutes for hardwood, which was not found in their environment. Walrus ivory provided the most durable and finely finished material for small objects. Caribou antler was more easily worked but tougher and more flexible, furnishing the best substance for knife handles and weapon components. Muskox horn could be softened, cut, and reshaped as an excellent substitute for softwood. Although bone was hard and brittle, the odd shapes of some bones suited a unique purpose. When men were not hunting, carving and grinding these materials must have provided a constant occupation.

Hunting was the first and most important task of an Independence camp. The interest and rewards of the small community were focused on this endeavour, which provided the exhilarations, dangers, and satisfactions of a life that depended directly on chasing and killing animals. All the capable men and boys in the community would have been hunters; all women must have hunted occasionally, and some probably hunted full time either from necessity or inclination. In addition to seeking their daily sustenance, hunters must have endeavoured to cache as much food as possible for the coming winter. A cache of meat could prove the difference between survival and death in the event that the winter brought unexpected distress. Whenever more animals were killed than were needed for immediate stocks, the surplus meat would have been carefully stored. The cold Arctic climate would make the actual preservation of meat simple but produce other complications: meat had to be butchered and stored in small enough packages to be recoverable during the winter, when extreme cold had turned the food to the consistency of stone. Cache locations had to be selected in areas that would not be buried beneath winter snow drifts and that could be located in the dark of the winter night. Finally, the stores had to be deeply buried in boulders to prevent foxes and wolves, and the occasional polar bear, from plundering their contents for an unexpected meal. Caches of driftwood and other fuel that the hunters had picked up during their summer wanderings may also have been made. With the coming of winter, a small local group could probably feel secure only if its territory were dotted with boulder-covered caches filled with meat and the fuel to cook it.

Hunting, caching food, and preparing winter clothing must have continued into the shortening days of autumn, as ice crept across the tundra ponds and squalls of snow drifted across the landscape. The selection of a wintering location would have been a crucial decision as the long winter night began to set in. A good location would be sheltered from the worst of the expected winter storms, in an area where wintering muskox herds could be expected, and where caches of food and fuel were accessible. More than one such camp might be needed during the long winter, but winter moves must have been so difficult that they would be avoided if possible.

A winter camp of the Independence people must have been all but invisible to a stranger. The dark tent, covered with heavy, black-haired muskox hides, would have been deeply banked with snow and much of the remainder covered with drift snow. We can imagine a snow-covered tent flap being pushed aside to allow a pair of men to emerge. Perhaps they are encouraged by calm moonlight or by the glow in the southern sky during the brief midday dusk of early winter to try their luck at hunting. The men and dogs move through a silent landscape, their breath pluming and the hard-drifted snow creaking beneath their feet. Shallow craters dug through the snow crust – signs of muskoxen attempting to feed on the vegetation below – are easily found by the dogs. The herd itself appears as a dark smudge against a distant hillside, but the dogs are loosed too soon and take up their own hunt, fuelled by the image of a warm, frost-smoking carcass. By the time that the breathless hunters arrive the herd has broken and run out of sight. Pursuit would be foolish with the light quickly fading; their own visions of fresh meat dying, the men talk over what to do next as the dogs limp back. One of last summer's caches can probably be found before total darkness descends. Just when they are convincing each other that they have missed it, the small cairn of boulders on the edge of a high terrace appears against the fading skyline. Using a loose boulder from the top of the pile, the frozen rocks are knocked apart and some chunks broken loose from the frozen mass of food within. The dogs are rewarded with scattered chips of frozen meat, and they lunge at a silent raven that has appeared from the dark sky and perched on a nearby rock.

The return of the hunters wakes up the silent camp. But instead of fresh muskox flesh, the men and dogs carry packs of frozen meat and fish chopped from the cache near the failed hunt. Children tumble out of the tent to slide on the hard snow, while a woman strikes sparks from flint and a small ball of pyrites kept in her sewing kit. Dried moss eventually catches fire, and a tiny flame flickers around the twigs of willow and shavings of driftwood collected with such pains during the previous summer. The tent is filled with smoke and frozen breath and shadows that jump against the frost crystals condensed on the walls since the last fire. Bones smashed at the last meal crackle and spit in the stone hearth, and the two small families gather around the flames that have so transformed their environment. Chunks of meat placed close to the fire begin to thaw; sharp knives quickly shave off the half-frozen food, and it is eaten as soon as human teeth are capable of chewing it. When the fuel runs out, the housewife picks pebbles from the hearth, and drops them hissing into the skin

Artist's conception of life in the interior of an Independence tent dwelling. It is difficult to imagine how such a frail shelter could protect the life of a family through the long night of a polar winter.

pot packed with snow and scraps of meat. Surprisingly quickly the mixture melts and begins to steam, producing the thin, lukewarm soup that is the main winter sustenance of every family. The pot is quickly drained, and the children again disappear outdoors while their elders watch the embers of the fast-dying fire and discuss the weather and their next hunt. The smoke hole in the roof is plugged with skins as the cold, briefly banished by the tiny fire, creeps back into the tent. The families retreat beneath their muskox hide blankets, and eventually even the children seek refuge from the cold and dark in the darker confines of home. The tent moves and creaks in a rising wind, the dogs curl into the snow as a light ground drift sifts across the landscape, and a silent aurora flares across the top of the sky. The camp will sleep for another day, or perhaps until hunger goads them once again to face the waking world.

Is this imagined way of life too stark and difficult to be credible? The winter life of the Independence people, as reconstructed here, is certainly well beyond the bounds of endurance known from any human group described by anthropologists or historians. Yet it is difficult to imagine how their winter lives could have been very different from this portrayal. They lived in an area so distant from other environments that a winter retreat to more congenial conditions was not possible. Their environment provided them with plentiful food and clothing but with only the barest minimum of fuel for winter fires. The hard-won fuel resources that they did accumulate must have provided only for small and occasional fires, enough to thaw food and melt ice for water but not to provide a heat source for human warmth. Such warmth had to be produced internally by the consumption of food and carefully conserved by warm clothing, blankets, and inactivity.

Eigil Knuth was the first to suggest that the Independence people may have passed the winter 'in a kind of torpor.' The months of winter darkness must have discouraged all but the most essential hunting, preventing women from sewing clothing and men from working at their crafts. We are forced to imagine a winter life devoted to amusing the children, singing or telling stories, thinking of the coming summer, and dreaming. Northern Canada used to teem with anecdotes of isolated White trappers who spent the winters in semi-hibernation, passing days or weeks at a time in dreams rather than in the reality of cold darkness and scarce food. The early Palaeo-Eskimos may have survived the High

Arctic only by adopting such a way of life as the ordinary custom for an entire society. How else can we interpret the archaeological evidence, which reveals the open hearths of winter dwellings containing charcoal and burnt bones from only a few small fires?

If the Independence people did survive in this way, compressing their activities into the summer months of constant daylight and then retreating into their dreams for several months a year, we must imagine a way of life that was as rich in the imagination as it was poor in material comforts. Perhaps it was the results of such a life, nurtured and developed over countless generations, that can eventually be seen in the extraordinary art of later Palaeo-Eskimo peoples.

But Could They Survive?

The way of life described in the previous section would have been not only arduous in the extreme but also desperately insecure. The tiny camp groups of winter must have been very vulnerable to any mishap or mistake: a hunter's broken leg; a heavy snowstorm that hid too many caches of meat and fuel; or a simple miscalculation of the amount of stored food needed for an unexpectedly long winter. Any of these, or of a dozen different sorts of incident, could easily result in the demise of an entire local band. The failure of such a band to arrive at a planned summer rendezvous must have been an all too common occurrence, and cannot have been unexpected.

How many such events could be supported by the Independence population before the entire way of life disappeared? Human social groups seem to require a population pool of a few hundred people in order to maintain themselves over long periods of time. The size of the Independence population is very difficult to judge from archaeological evidence because most of the vast region that they inhabited has not been thoroughly searched. The small size of their settlements, however, the evidence that most of these represent only temporary camps, and the fact that large stretches of the country show little evidence of occupation combine to suggest that the population was extremely small and scattered: perhaps two or three hundred people spread over a million square kilometres.

The specialization of many Independence groups on muskox hunting must have contributed to their insecurity. The biology of muskoxen is rather poorly known, but recent populations have proved very vulnerable to overhunting as well as to natural disasters. In the winter of 1973, for example, an autumn storm of freezing rain formed an unbreakable ice crust over the snow and vegetation of Bathurst Island in the central High Arctic. Most of the large muskox population of the island starved during the winter, and a decade later the herds had still not recovered their original size. Muskoxen, like other herd animals, are subject to infectious diseases, although the consequences of such disease are not well known.

The Independence muskox hunters had to accept the possibility that local herds could quickly disappear. Survival in such cases would have depended on mobility over long distances: being capable of moving one's entire family and belongings over hundreds of kilometres; knowing the geography and hunting conditions of distant areas; and most important, having social relationships with distant peoples in whose territory one might find refuge in time of need. Whatever strategies local bands used to cope with such disasters, and despite the fact that many such bands probably did not survive the consequences of inevitable mishaps, there is growing evidence that the Independence way of life did survive for a remarkably long time.

Independence I and Independence II

The coasts of the High Arctic are lined with skeins of ancient beaches, parallel strings of gravel running close together around steep headlands and spreading apart in shallow bays. Crossing the beaches from the present shore is like mounting a long series of steps, each step a beach formed in the past. Since the Ice Age, most High Arctic coasts have been rising from the sea, as the land recovers from the down-warping caused by its burden of glacial ice. The weight of the glaciers caused the earth's crust to sink, and it then springs back very slowly; each beach represents a stage in this process. Flat and covered with dry, hard-packed gravel, raised beaches make excellent camping locations as well as walking paths as fine as nature provides anywhere on earth.

For the archaeologist, they also provide a measure of age for the remains left behind by people who lived on these beaches in the distant past. Arctic peoples usually camp on the beach closest to the coast, where they have immediate access to either open water or sea ice. Since each raised beach is older than its lower neighbour, the remains of camps on the highest beaches can be expected to be the oldest. This was the situation encountered by Eigil Knuth when he explored the fiords of northern Greenland. He found that the meagre remains left by Inuit travelling through the area were found on the lowest beaches, adjacent to the present shore. The midpassage tent rings of the Independence culture, on the other hand, were scattered along the old raised beaches, far above the shore. Knuth was tempted to imagine these ruins as 'fossils,' which could be dated in the same way that geologists date the animal remains associated with these geological features: 'The stone circles laid by man had also risen and now were not only seemingly but actually fossil or subfossil phenomena high up, sunk in clay as hard as cement and worn by water. Among mussel and snail shells they lay like skeletons of the dwellings of some animal species suddenly emerged – evidence of the increase of fauna during a definite geological period.'

The beach levels also provided the first hint that the Independence culture comprised two distinct occupations of northern Greenland: the larger group of structures were found on beaches eleven or twelve metres above present sea level but there was another distinct group at only five to six metres elevation. The implied difference in age between the two groups was confirmed by radiocarbon dating of charcoal and animal bones recovered from hearths. That from the upper-level structures dated to the centuries between 2500 and 2000 BC, while material from the structures located at the lower level produced dates almost 2,000 years more recent. Knuth also noted differences in the forms of the structures located on the two sets of beaches and in the artifacts recovered from them. Concluding that there had been two major and ancient occupations of far northern Greenland, he named the earlier occupation Independence I and the later Independence II.

Evidence of the same two periods of occupation has been found in most areas of the High Arctic that have been searched by archaeologists. In most coastal areas the two sets of sites are separated by several metres in elevation, and the beaches between these two levels usually show no traces of human use. Does this mean that there were two early Palaeo-Eskimo occupations of the High Arctic, perhaps each lasting only for a few generations and separated by a millennium or more when the area was not inhabited? The interpretation of two short-term occupations, each ending in the disappearance of the local Palaeo-Eskimo population, seems consistent with evidence suggesting the fragility and insecurity of

Strings of raised gravel beaches rise like
broad stairs from the present coast. These
beaches on southern Ellesmere Island
carry the remains of camps relating to both
Independence I (at twenty-two metres
above sea level) and Independence II (at
ten metres above sea level) people.

The remains of an Independence II
dwelling lie on a Devon Island beach.

the Independence people's way of life. Perhaps the animal resources of the most northerly Arctic regions were simply too meagre and unstable to support long-term human occupation in the region, even by a people as adaptable as the Palaeo-Eskimos.

A Long Tradition

Recent discoveries on the far northern islands of the Canadian Arctic have changed this interpretation. Over the past decades, archaeologists have searched the coasts and valleys of northern Ellesmere and Axel Heiberg islands, the portion of Arctic Canada adjacent to the Pearyland region of northern Greenland. They have recorded hundreds of archaeological features, and many of the occupation sites discovered relate to the Independence occupation of the area. Many can be assigned to either Independence I or Independence II, but the affiliation of a number of others is not so clear, and various hints suggest that they might represent occupation between the two major periods. This suspicion was confirmed in 1989 with the discovery and excavation of the Rivendell site in the interior of northern Ellesmere Island. The site produced not only artifacts that showed a mixture of Independence I and II characteristics but several radiocarbon dates that placed it squarely between the two previously documented occupations. With the other undated sites that furnished similar ranges of artifacts, the Rivendell site affords a new perspective on the Independence occupation of the extreme High Arctic. It suggests that, in at least some regions, there was occupational continuity between the Independence I and II periods.

The Rivendell site is located at the western end of Lake Hazen, the great freshwater lake that lies across the northern interior of Ellesmere Island. The broad valley in which Lake Hazen lies, surrounded by ice-capped mountains that protect it from the winds sweeping off the Arctic Ocean, is noted for its warm summer temperatures. It has been called an 'Arctic oasis,' a huge area where the vegetation is lusher than elsewhere in the High Arctic, rich in muskoxen, caribou, hares, and waterfowl. Lake Hazen and the rapid-strewn river that connects it to the sea support a dense population of arctic char. Perhaps in this unusually rich environment Independence people were able to survive the catastrophes and environmental changes that may have periodically devastated their relatives living in less favoured zones. The Hazen Valley may have been one of several areas of refuge from which Independence people could periodically expand their occupation to more desolate regions and thus maintain continuity of their unique culture and adaptation over a lengthy period.

Our archaeological knowledge now suggests that the way of life first developed by the Independence people about 2500 BC survived in the extreme High Arctic for at least 2,000 years. To gain perspective on such a length of time, we might note that it is roughly the same duration as the history of Christianity, or from Julius Caesar's time to the present. A cultural tradition that could survive for such a period on the far fringes of the habitable world must be considered remarkably successful. Considering our reconstruction of a way of life so meagre that it would not be contemplated by the Inuit or other Arctic peoples, the endurance of the Independence culture is all the more striking.

Hunters of the Low Arctic

While the Independence people were first encountering the muskox herds of the High Arctic, other Palaeo-Eskimo groups explored more southerly regions of Arctic North America. By at least 2000 BC, these newcomers had begun to develop ways of life suited to each of the distinctive environmental areas between Alaska and Greenland. Archaeologists working in each major region know the early Palaeo-Eskimos by different names: the Denbigh people in Alaska; Pre-Dorset in Canada; and Saqqaq in southern Greenland. These diverse names are mainly a reflection of the history of Arctic research and should not disguise the fact that all of the Palaeo-Eskimo groups across Arctic North America must have shared a very similar culture and traditions.

Our knowledge of these populations – when they first arrived in each area, the size of their social groups, the nature of their annual round of activities – is even vaguer and more uncertain than our knowledge of the High Arctic Independence people. This may seem strange, since the archaeological sites that they left are generally larger and more productive of artifacts, and a greater number of them have been excavated. The answer to the apparent paradox lies in a combination of factors. For one, these groups inhabited Low Arctic regions in which most of the surface is thickly covered in tundra vegetation. The meagre remains of early Palaeo-Eskimo settlements, readily apparent from a distance on the barren beaches of the High Arctic, are effectively hidden by the tundra.

When sites are found, it is often by chance during the excavation of a more recent structure. Another problem arises from the topography of many Low Arctic regions, in which rocky outcrops and wetlands limit the areas suitable for establishing a camp. Level, dry, sheltered locations that provide easy access to a nearby resource are likely to have been occupied many times over a period of centuries. Such sites are built of many layers of individual occupation, the later inhabitants taking apart and rebuilding the dwelling remains left by their predecessors. For archaeologists digging such a site, the remains of any single occupation is difficult to distinguish from those older and younger. Most Palaeo-Eskimo sites in the Low Arctic yield many more artifacts than do Independence sites but less information on dwellings, the size of individual social units, the number of occupation sites in an area, or the time at which a particular occupation occurred.

Problems of interpretation are increased by the much greater range of economic choices available to most early occupants of Low Arctic areas than to their compatriots in the High Arctic. Animal populations were more numerous and more diverse, and there was a greater range of opportunities for exploiting them. On top of this, the warmer conditions and the acids produced by Low Arctic vegetation have combined to destroy the animal bones discarded by the occupants at many sites, leaving archaeologists only large collections of chipped-stone tools from which to interpret an ancient way of life.

For these reasons, the archaeological reconstruction of Palaeo-Eskimo life styles in Low Arctic regions is often limited to interpretations of the subsistence activities of these groups: what animals they hunted, what weapons they used, and perhaps at what time of year they conducted these activities. Beyond this, we can only assume that most of their culture, technology, and traditions were generally similar to those of the Independence people whom we described earlier in this chapter. Yet the relatively large size of their sites, the rich middens of animal bones that are sometimes preserved, and the fact that these groups lived in areas where the midwinter night was either short or non-existent assure us that their ways of life must have been considerably more comfortable and secure than those we imagine for the Independence people.

CHAPTER 5

The Great Exploration

When ancestral Palaeo-Eskimos first encountered the tundra coasts of Alaska, they had discovered the last major environment on earth that was unoccupied by humans. They had probably arrived in the area by crossing the winter ice from the nearby Siberian shore, a journey that can be undertaken without ever travelling more than twenty kilometres from land. They had most likely come to search for animals in the country that loomed above the eastern horizon. They cannot have known they were at the beginning of an eastward trek that would take their descendants across several thousand kilometres and over 150 degrees of longitude, almost half way around the northern world.

This journey was probably accomplished fairly quickly on an archaeological time scale, perhaps within a few generations. In fact, the radiocarbon dates that are our primary means of detecting the ages of Palaeo-Eskimo occupations are earlier on sites in the eastern Arctic than in Alaska. Given the imprecision and interpretation problems associated with the radiocarbon dating technique, this does not prove that the Palaeo-Eskimo came from the eastern Arctic; it probably does indicate, however, that the occupation of the entire North American Arctic was accomplished within a very short period.

The exploration and settlement of such a vast area defies our imagination. The process comprised hundreds of individual events, decisions, adaptations, and courageous explorations. We must imagine several independent bands of people moving east at different times and for different reasons, gradually learning the geography and environment of northern

The tundra coast of eastern Siberia, where vast herds of reindeer migrate along shores teeming with fish and sea mammals, is probably where hunters developed the techniques necessary for Arctic life. Very similar but unoccupied lands lay in Alaska, clearly visible from the hilltops in this picture.

North America and passing that knowledge through an ever widening and ever loosening network of relatives. Eventually the process created a thin scatter of human population over millions of square kilometres of tundra and sea ice, each local band establishing its own traditions and customs tied to its own well-loved homeland.

What must it have been like to take part in this process? Can an event of such complexity and such extent be described in a fashion that makes sense of such a vast human experience? Perhaps by collapsing the process, by imagining it as if it occurred in only a half-dozen steps, we might contrive to understand the immensity of the undertaking.

Alaska

East Cape, the most easterly point of Asia, extends a narrow, rocky finger from the tundras of Chukotka into the waters of the Bering Sea. A few kilometres offshore lies a long mountainous island, Big Diomede, marking the half-way point to North America. The American continent itself is easily seen from the heights above the cape, and even from beach level the highlands behind Cape Prince of Wales loom above the horizon in summer mirages. The first hunters to reach this part of Siberia knew that another land lay just beyond the horizon, and the first tentative explorations probably took place within a few years.

The first impressions of Alaska must have occurred on what is now known as Seward Peninsula, a great tongue of rolling, tundra-covered land extending west toward Bering Strait. Relieved at coming ashore from the constant glare, noise, and danger of spring ice, the first explorers must have been comforted to realize how similar this land was to their homeland. In the long spring sunlight the lush tundra was alive with caribou, recently arrived on their annual migration from the distant forests to their calving grounds and summer range near the Arctic coast. The nests of ducks, geese, and swans surrounded every tundra pond, and the rivers swarmed with migrating fish; no one would go hungry in the new country.

The explorers may have stayed for only a few days, or perhaps for an entire summer, before returning home. On the tundras of northeastern Siberia, their accounts of a rich and unoccupied land to the east would have been discussed whenever there was famine or when disputes arose over access to hunting territories. When a particularly menacing dispute occurred, one group's decision to try to make a life in the new land cannot

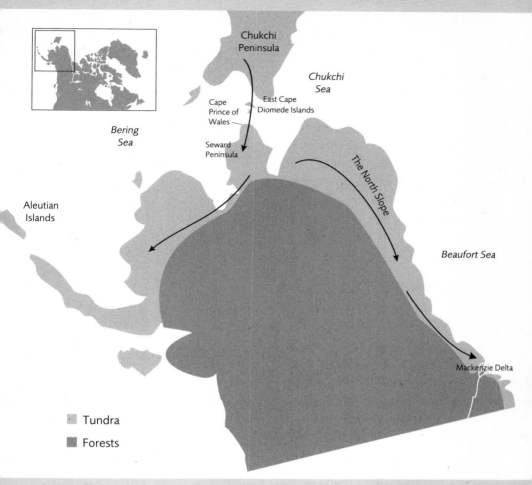

Chukchi
Peninsula

Chukchi
Sea

East Cape
Diomede Islands

Cape
Prince of
Wales

Bering
Sea

Seward
Peninsula

Aleutian
Islands

The North Slope

Beaufort Sea

Mackenzie Delta

Tundra
Forests

MAP 5.1
Expansion of Palaeo-Eskimo occupation
from Siberia to Alaska

have been a surprise. People and dogs could have crossed to the half-way islands in one or two long spring days, carrying everything needed to make a new beginning. A day or so of rest, another day finding a way across the leads of open water caused by tidal currents swirling around the Diomede Islands, and another day of walking across shifting and booming ice, and the first Palaeo-Eskimo settlers had arrived in the New World.

With food so plentiful, the first summer would have been devoted to exploring the country in search of a territory where the group could spend the coming winter. As the winter approached they would have followed the caribou, now heavy with fat and with hides in prime condition for making clothing, east toward the edge of the interior forest. Somewhere near the first outliers of spruce trees they must have had their first encounter with the people of the forest, who were carrying out their own autumn caribou hunt. The meeting must have been wary, with neither party quite certain that the other was fully human. From a distance, each would have noted clothing, hair styles, and facial tattoos that were alien to any known in their own band's experience or history; if they came within voice range, they would have found that each spoke an unintelligible language. If a skirmish developed, the Dene Indians' superior knowledge of the country and will to defend their homeland must have been evenly balanced by the Palaeo-Eskimos' superior weapons – bows and arrows – and their need to find a homeland. This first encounter probably established the pattern for hundreds of others that were to occur during the coming centuries along the forest border between Bering Strait and Hudson Bay. These confrontations probably resulted in the Dene retiring closer to the forest and the Palaeo-Eskimos retreating farther into the tundra. The zone beyond the tree line, where small islands of spruce forest were scattered in decreasing size across the tundra, must have become a no man's land, which individual bands could breach only when a battle seemed necessary or if trading relationships were established with long-time neighbours.

If they had been lucky enough to make a major kill of caribou, probably at a place where the migrating herds bunched up to cross a river, the immigrants would have built winter houses nearby and prepared for the season of cold and darkness. Their houses were rectangular, about three by four metres and dug slightly into the earth; the roofs, rising from the four-sided structure with rounded corners that made them appear

The tree line, the zone between tundra
and interior forests, marked the boundary
between ancestral Dene and Palaeo-
Eskimo zones of occupation.

almost conical, were supported by the abundant driftwood of rivers running from the forest, covered with hides and buried in turf. There was probably enough driftwood to keep a fire constantly alight in the central hearth, providing light and heat throughout the winter. Their food supply could be supplemented by winter hunting of caribou and by fishing through the ice of lakes and rivers. The new land may have supplied everything that they required to spend a comfortable first winter, but the newcomers must have eagerly awaited the bounties of spring: the endless strings of caribou threading their way across the thawing snow, the cacophony of waterfowl, and the first runs of fish in the melting rivers.

Summer may have brought further exploration. Some of the first group of immigrants may have wandered south through the coastal tundras of western Alaska, eventually settling along the salmon-rich rivers of the Bering Sea coast. Others could have hunted northward, soon discovering the great coastal plain of North Alaska. Stretching over 1,000 kilometres from Point Hope to the Mackenzie Delta and up to 300 kilometres in width, the region now known as the North Slope is a tundra plain separated from the forested interior by a range of mountains 2,000 metres high or more. Each year the caribou herds that calve and graze on the summer tundra are funnelled along mountain valleys and through a few narrow passes in order to reach their wintering range in the forests. These defiles form natural traps, which can be easily exploited by human hunters, and the early Palaeo-Eskimos soon established themselves at the most strategic locations, developing a way of life that must have survived for millennia.

Each spring groups probably followed the migrating caribou north to their summering grounds on the coastal plain, and some may have established summer homes on the shores of the Chukchi and Beaufort seas. Seals could be hunted from the shore ice, and perhaps a few groups built small hunting boats of a traditional kayak-like design for inshore sealing in open water. The archaeological site at Cape Denbigh, where the existence of the Palaeo-Eskimos first came to light in Alaska, is probably the remains of a small summer coastal hunting camp at the western end of the North Alaskan coastal plain.

The Mackenzie Coast

As groups drifted east, taking advantage of unfished rivers and unhunted animals, they found the Alaskan coastal plain narrowing. Summer caribou hunting may have become easier in this region, as the herds were more densely concentrated in a narrow strip between the mountains and the sea. The area used for the entire yearly round of activities, from winter hunting in the mountain passes to summer sealing on the coast, could be traversed in a few days of walking down one of the small tumbling rivers of what is now the northern Yukon. It was very apparent, however, that this was the eastern end of the environmental region that they knew as their home. To the east, the land quickly dropped away to a broad, flat valley stretching almost to the limit of vision, filled with a huge meandering river split into countless winding channels.

The Mackenzie River has built one of the world's great deltas, over fifty kilometres wide and 200 kilometres long. Along with silt eroded from the northern prairies and drift trees quarried from the riverbanks of northern British Columbia, it brings a sub-Arctic environment to the Arctic coast. The delta is a maze of interlocking channels, lakes, and ponds, set into a landscape of permanently frozen silt. In Palaeo-Eskimo times it was covered by a dense spruce forest, except for a possible fringe of tundra along the outermost islands. The river channels and lakes of the delta are some of the most productive fishing waters in Arctic North America, and by the time that the Palaeo-Eskimo first saw the forested valley it had long been occupied by Dene Indians. We have no idea how the Palaeo-Eskimos coped with this new and alien environment. Until archaeological sites are found, we should perhaps assume that some groups eventually crossed it simply in order to investigate hunting conditions on the rolling, tundra-covered hills that could be distantly glimpsed on the far side. To a people who had few if any boats, the summer delta was an impenetrable maze. Forays into the area and eventual crossings were probably limited to winter and spring, when the entire area was bridged by ice. We may imagine that people skirted the outer fringe of the delta, perhaps at a season when Indian occupants had retreated to the denser forests away from the outer coast.

The first groups to cross the Mackenzie Delta discovered themselves in an environment quite different from that to the west. The mountains that had always defined their Alaskan and Siberian homelands, channelling the movements of the caribou and separating their territory from those of forest dwellers, had now been left behind. To the east there stretched a flat and limitless country, bounded by the Arctic coast and by

The Mackenzie Delta, along the eastern
foothills of the mountains, marks a major
environmental boundary between the
Western and Central Arctic.

a tree line that quickly fell away to the south. The ever broadening plain between forest and coast was clothed in lush tundra vegetation, rutted with the deep trails of migrating caribou. It must also have been dotted with animals of which the first Palaeo-Eskimos to reach the region had heard only in legend.

The lowlands along the coast of the Beaufort Sea had not been glaciated during the last Ice Age, enabling animals to thrive there during the period. Like the adjacent regions of North Alaska, and extending in Ice Age times across the Bering Land Bridge to eastern Siberia, these plains had been home to herds of Arctic animals as diverse as caribou, antelope, horses, bison, muskoxen, and mammoths. Most of these animals were too vulnerable to changing environmental conditions and the presence of human hunters, and became extinct at the end of the Ice Age around 10,000 years ago. The coastal plain east of the Mackenzie River, however, provided conditions that allowed some of these animals to survive post-glacial conditions. The deep silts that cover the region support a shrubby tundra that is today rich in grass, dwarf willow, birch, and alder; this area may have been particularly lush in the warm period following the Ice Age, while permafrost and cold winds off the Beaufort Sea prevented the establishment of forest conditions. In contrast with northern Alaska or Siberia, the area remained relatively free of human predators; northern Indian groups concentrated their hunting relatively close to the forest limit.

The immigrants cannot have been in the new country for more than a few hours or days before they saw the first species of unknown animal. Even at a great distance, the small group of black dots was obviously something other than the tan-coloured caribou, brown or white bears, and grey wolves with which they were familiar. The first strange animals seen were probably muskoxen, very vulnerable to human hunters and probably long extinct in the country through which they and their ancestors had travelled. They may have been bison, larger animals with straighter horns than the plains bison known from the past centuries. These northern relatives of today's bison had probably been hunted to extinction in the lands farther west but continued to survive in the coastal plain and adjacent islands of the western Canadian Arctic. The exotic animals may even have included mammoths. Although there is no evidence that mammoths survived so recently in this area, they persisted on isolated islands off the Arctic coast of Siberia until hunters related to the Palaeo-Eskimo reached their refuge. It is possible that a small population of New World mammoths may have found refuge in the same tundras that allowed the arctic bison to survive until the past few millennia.

Although bison and perhaps mammoths must have been spectacular animals to the early Palaeo-Eskimos, they probably existed in too small numbers and too limited an area to provide an important food resource. Muskoxen, however, must have grazed in large numbers over the tundras now encountered by the Palaeo-Eskimos. Easily hunted by people with dogs and bows and living throughout the year on the open tundra, this newly discovered animal must have become one of the most basic elements in the adaptation that the immigrants made to the central Canadian Arctic.

The Barren Grounds

The eastern boundary of the Mackenzie coastal plain was probably marked for the Palaeo-Eskimos, as it is today, by the Smoking Hills. Plumes of sulphurous smoke rising far into the sky can be seen from a great distance and can occasionally be smelled as far away as the Mackenzie River mouth, 300 kilometres to the west. When the first explorers reached the source on the shores of Franklin Bay, just to the east of Cape Bathurst, they found smoke and steam belching from dozens of red and yellow vents scattered along several kilometres of sea cliffs. The Smoking Hills are an evil-smelling, grossly polluted, and obviously hazardous place. We must imagine that this bizarre phenomenon not only featured as a geographic marker for the early Palaeo-Eskimos but also represented supernatural power and danger. It was probably an area to be avoided whenever possible, while playing an important role in the mythology and world view of the bands that lived within occasional sight of the mysterious smoke.

East of the Smoking Hills lay a great triangle of rock and tundra, extending almost 2,000 kilometres to the coast of Hudson Bay. This is the area known today as the Barren Grounds, a broad expanse of Canadian Shield rocks and the last major area to emerge from beneath the continental glaciers of the Ice Age. When the Palaeo-Eskimos first saw them, the Barren Grounds were dotted with herds of resident muskoxen and refilled each spring with endless streams of migratory caribou. The rivers and lakes were thick with char and trout, and their banks lined with nesting waterfowl. Although we have not found the sites left by the first

The Smoking Hills, along the eastern coast
of the Cape Bathurst Peninsula, must have
been an important geographical marker for
the first Palaeo-Eskimo explorers of Arctic
Canada.

Palaeo-Eskimo explorers of the area, we know from more recent occupations that they must have thrived, and we can easily imagine the way of life that they adopted.

The key to life on the Barren Grounds has always been a knowledge of the rivers. Rising in the high country of the far interior, the great rivers now known as Coppermine, Back, Thelon, and Kazan radiate north and east to the Arctic coast and Hudson Bay. These are not smoothly flowing streams but plunging torrents filled with rapids and cataracts as they drop through a rock-ribbed landscape. Occasionally their courses are obstructed by natural dams, and the rivers form long and narrow lakes as they fill their valleys before overflowing the obstruction. Knowledge of the fishing conditions at cascading rapids, at lake inlets and outlets, and in the short stretches of placidly flowing river is important to anyone exploiting the rich resources of these rivers. Awareness of these features is even more crucial to hunters of caribou.

Most Barren Grounds rivers lie across the paths followed by caribou on their spring migration from the forest and on their autumn return south. The movements of some of the largest caribou herds in the Arctic world are channelled by the rivers and lakes of the Barren Grounds, as the animals seek traditional crossing places at fords and narrows. For any Barren Grounds hunter, the most important time of year has always been the autumn migration, when fattened caribou converge into enormous herds and drift south toward the forest. The traditional hunters' goal was to predict the place where such a herd bunched up at a difficult river crossing, to wait in ambush, and then to kill as many as possible of the milling and frightened animals. The caribou were butchered, their hides removed to make winter clothing, and the meat stored in large, boulder-covered caches near the crossing. The hunters then waited for the next herd. If they had selected their hunting location well and the herds arrived as predicted, the hunters could easily amass a winter supply of food for a band of several small families.

Winter would be spent at a sheltered location near the food supply, perhaps in one of the small patches of spruce trees that lay in protected valleys far north of the continuous forest. The winter dwelling was probably a conical tent covered with caribou or muskox skins, supported by spruce poles and heavily banked with snow. Heat, light, and cooking were provided by a central fire, which burned local spruce wood if it was

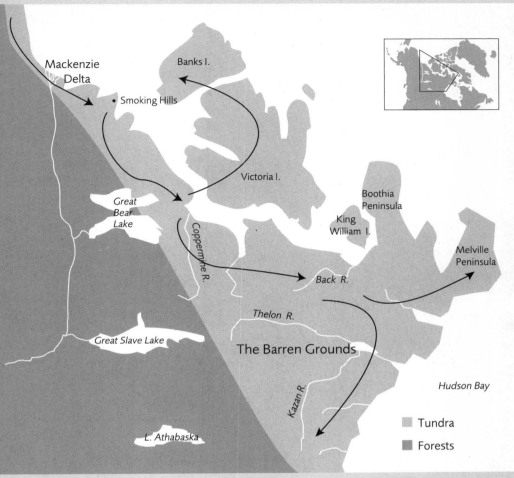

MAP 5.2
Expansion of Palaeo-Eskimo occupation
from Alaska to the Barren Grounds

The Coppermine River, flowing through
the western edge of the Barren Grounds, is
the first of the rivers which channel the
huge herds of caribou migrating between
the forests and the Arctic coast.

available, driftwood collected from rivers that had their headwaters within the forests, or the willow and birch shrubs that grew in sheltered areas across the region. Since most of the Barren Grounds area lies close to or south of the Arctic Circle, the long midwinter night of higher latitudes would not have been a problem for local groups. The darkest day of midwinter provided at least a few hours of twilight by which a hunter could track a muskox herd, find a cache of meat from the previous summer's hunt, or chop a hole through lake ice in order to jig for trout. For people whose traditions had been formed in the high-latitude tundras of North Alaska and Siberia, the Barren Grounds of the central Arctic must have seemed a utopia.

The lengthening sunlight of spring may have brought hunger, as food caches emptied and the beginning of the spring thaw made hunting and travelling difficult. The season of scarcity came to an end when long lines of pregnant caribou cows began to appear, advancing purposefully northward down the frozen water courses and along the eskers, the great fossil rivers of gravel winding like snakes across the Barren Grounds. Summers may have been spent following the caribou to their calving grounds near the Arctic coast or in amassing stores of dried fish at choice fishing spots along the rivers. Some groups may have summered along the Arctic or Hudson Bay coasts, attracted to the shore by the relative lack of biting flies and by the possibility of obtaining seal meat, blubber, and waterproof skins. The summer hunt, however, was conditioned by the need to be at a crossing place in time to intercept the southward migration of caribou. If the hunters arrived in time at their wintering place and the herds arrived as expected, another year of life in the Barren Grounds was assured.

Within a very few generations, the Palaeo-Eskimos must have known every river, every esker, and every caribou trail in the Barren Grounds. Small bands of a few related families had established winter quarters in every location that provided a source of food and shelter, and a widespread network would have passed knowledge and news through strings of neighbouring bands. The population probably remained very small and dispersed, perhaps a few hundred people scattered over half a million square kilometres of landscape. Some of the more southerly groups may have skirmished or occasionally established wary relationships of trade and mutual help with the Dene Indian peoples of the neighbouring forests. Some of the western bands may have retained contact with the Palaeo-Eskimo groups that continued to occupy the Mackenzie coastal plain to the west. Still others used the Barren Grounds only as a bridge to further explorations, across the islands of the Arctic Archipelago.

The Western Islands

The immense caribou herds of the Barren Grounds do not stop their northward migrations at the Arctic coast. The pregnant cows that lead the spring migration appear to be following an urge to bear their calves as far as possible from the forest edge and from the wolves and grizzly bears to which infant caribou are easy prey. Later in the season, caribou move farther north in order to escape the biting insects that infest the interior. In traditional times, large herds travelled each spring across the forty kilometres of ice separating Victoria Island from the mainland. The two great northward-stretching arms of the Arctic mainland to the east, Boothia Peninsula and Melville Peninsula, supported sizable caribou herds and were separated by only a kilometre or two of frozen sea from King William, Somerset, and Baffin islands. It is easy to imagine how Palaeo-Eskimo caribou hunters, following the summer movements of their prey, began to explore the islands of the central Arctic.

The Low Arctic islands form an interlinked mosaic, any part of which can be reached from its neighbour in less than a day's walk, and in many cases in less than an hour's walk, across sea ice that is stable for eight months of the year. None of the channels would have formed a barrier to the movements of either animals or early Palaeo-Eskimo explorers. As they moved through the archipelago, however, the explorers must have encountered a number of distinct environments that encouraged them to develop new and more efficient adaptations.

The large western islands, Victoria and Banks, were probably the first to be explored. These islands are wide expanses of rolling, prairie-like country, very similar to the adjacent western regions of the Barren Grounds and Mackenzie coast. The newcomers would have found exceptional hunting among resident herds of caribou, muskoxen, and probably a few bison, none of which had previously encountered human hunters. Like the traditional Inuit, they would have discovered the autumn trap that Barren Ground caribou had entered when they migrated north across the spring ice to Victoria Island. When it came time to retreat south to the forest, the

The central portion of the Arctic Archipelago is a maze of islands and peninsulas,
locked together by sea ice that can be
crossed by animals and human hunters for
most of the year.

caribou found that they were separated from the mainland by open channels and were forced to mill about at the crossing areas for a month or more before the autumn ice froze to a thickness that could safely carry them. The kills made at such natural traps must have easily encouraged the first winterings on the Arctic islands.

Eventually these bands must have explored farther north, crossing the narrow channel separating them from Banks Island to the west. With gently rolling hills and lush green tundra, Banks Island now supports over 40,000 muskoxen, a population far denser than in any other Arctic region. Then, as now, a hunter standing on the crest of a ridge or at the edge of a broad, shallow valley would have seen a landscape dotted in every direction with herds of animals. From the northern coast of Banks Island, explorers could see land across Parry Channel and may have observed muskoxen or caribou making the crossing. Melville Island, eighty kilometres north, is another muskox-rich island and may have been a gateway to the islands of the High Arctic.

Other bands, hunting along the southern coast of Banks Island on a very clear summer day, may have seen something more startling. The distant plume of white smoke rising from the Smoking Hills, far to the southwest across the open sea, must have been familiar from legend if not from experience. It may have encouraged travellers to make winter crossings over the almost 200 kilometres of sea ice separating Banks Island from Cape Bathurst and eventually to forge links with the peoples of the Mackenzie coast. Such links are apparent in the artifacts of later Palaeo-Eskimo occupants of Banks and Victoria Islands and may date to the time of the earliest immigrants.

The Eastern Islands

Fury and Hecla Strait is only a few kilometres wide, but it marks the boundary between two major environmental zones. To the south, the low gravel ridges of Melville Peninsula extend from the northeastern corner of the Barren Grounds and are a typical part of the central Arctic. To the north lies Baffin Island, rising gradually to the glacier-capped mountains that form its sheer northeastern coast. Off this coast lie Baffin Bay, Davis Strait, and the Labrador Sea, a corner of the Atlantic Ocean surrounded on three sides by mountainous lands: Baffin, Devon, and Ellesmere islands, Labrador, and Greenland. This is the eastern Arctic, a more rugged

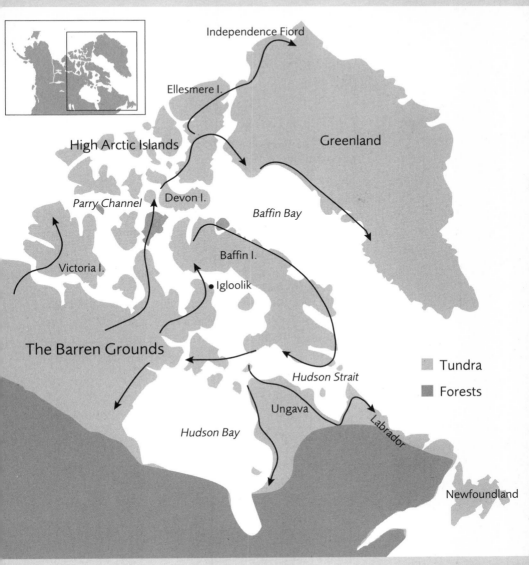

Independence Fiord

Ellesmere I.

Greenland

High Arctic Islands

Parry Channel

Devon I.

Baffin Bay

Victoria I.

Baffin I.

• Igloolik

The Barren Grounds

Hudson Strait

Ungava

Labrador

Hudson Bay

Newfoundland

Tundra

Forests

MAP 5.3
Expansion of Palaeo-Eskimo occupation
through the eastern Arctic

country than the plains to the west and an environment in which maritime conditions and resources are much more important than those of the land.

The traditional Inuit community of Igloolik lies on a small island of the same name in Fury and Hecla Strait. The remains of Palaeo-Eskimo settlements that are probably as old as any known from elsewhere in the Arctic lie on the bare gravel of the fossil beaches that rise like steps from the current shore of the island. The people who lived in these ancient settlements, however, had developed a pattern of hunting quite different from that of the Palaeo-Eskimo caribou hunters of the central Arctic or the Independence muskox hunters of the most northerly islands.

The first people to live at Igloolik did hunt the caribou that then, as now, must have grazed Melville Peninsula in the summer months. But Igloolik is famous not for its caribou but for the sea mammals concentrated in the adjacent strait, where currents maintain areas of thin ice and open water throughout the year. Seal, walrus, beluga, and narwhal are common in the area during the summer, and both seal and walrus winter in Fury and Hecla Strait. When restricted to narrow leads or small ponds of open water, these wintering animals are relatively easy prey for humans hunting from the adjacent ice. Pods of small whales are also occasionally trapped in tiny pools surrounded by encroaching ice, where they are very vulnerable to hunters with harpoons.

The early Palaeo-Eskimos at Igloolik did have harpoons and were capable of taking the sea mammals that teemed in the waters surrounding their island. The harpoon is an ingenious weapon, with a detachable head designed to stick into the flesh of a sea mammal and tied to a line by which the hunter can retrieve both harpoon head and prey. The handle is usually loosely attached to the line, so it too can be retrieved. Harpoons are the only weapons capable of efficiently hunting seals, walrus, or whales, and they seem to have been invented by several peoples who developed maritime hunting adaptations during the millennia following the last Ice Age. The small and relatively simple harpoons that the Palaeo-Eskimos used were probably based on a design invented either in Siberia or by the early maritime hunting peoples of eastern Asia. The design may have been kept alive in the culture of the caribou-hunting Palaeo-Eskimos of the central Arctic, as sealing weapons occasionally used during summer visits to coastal areas. When these people arrived in a region where marine animals could be easily hunted with harpoons thrown or thrust from the ice edge, there must have been a surge in harpoon making and design changes to accommodate animals as large as walrus or narwhal.

Taking such large and potentially dangerous animals with very simple equipment must have involved a great deal of audacity and learning through sad experience. Nevertheless, the reward was a more productive and more assured harvest of meat than that obtained from a hunt based on predicting the movements of wandering land mammals. The hunt also supplied valuable skins, ivory, and blubber. Once the early Palaeo-Eskimos had learned the mysteries of the ice-edge environment and developed the equipment and techniques to exploit it, they had opened a gate to the coastal regions of the eastern Arctic. Here, on the fringes of the North Atlantic, they were able to develop larger and denser populations, and probably a richer and more secure way of life, than had been possible for their caribou- and muskox-hunting relatives of more continental regions. It also allowed them to explore new hunting grounds along the sea-facing coasts of the eastern Arctic and to expand to a new range of environments.

Labrador

The coastline of Baffin Island provided ample opportunities for people who had developed the techniques of coastal ice-hunting. The south coast of the island must have been particularly attractive, as the steep, indented shore and ferocious tidal currents of Hudson Strait combined to create ideal conditions for inshore sea mammal hunting. This area has produced some of the largest archaeological collections of early Palaeo-Eskimo artifacts, probably reflecting the productivity of the area and the density of the human population.

Local groups must have quickly expanded along this coast, and they seem to have crossed Hudson Strait quickly to occupy its southern shore, in what is now northern Québec and Labrador. The crossing was probably accomplished on the winter ice, using as stepping stones the complex of islands scattered across northeastern Hudson Bay. The same set of islands could also be used to travel to the western coast of Hudson Bay and thus complete the circuit that their ancestors had begun when they left the Barren Grounds. This circuit – from Southampton Island north to Melville Peninsula and northern Baffin Island, then along the eastern coast of Baffin Island to Hudson Strait and back across northern

The rich coastal resources of Labrador and Greenland led the early Palaeo-Eskimos into sub-Arctic environments, where open water replaced the sea ice to which their ancestors had adapted their way of life.

Hudson Bay – seems to have encompassed the most prolific Palaeo-Eskimo populations of the Canadian Arctic over the next few millennia.

The southern shores of Hudson Strait gave the early Palaeo-Eskimos access to the sub-Arctic coasts that stretched south along the eastern side of Hudson Bay and the Atlantic coast of Labrador. The forested regions of both these coasts were occupied by Indian groups, maritime-adapted peoples who were distinctly different from the ancestral Dene whom the Palaeo-Eskimos had known in the regions west of Hudson Bay. The Palaeo-Eskimos seem to have rapidly occupied the portions of these coasts that extended north of the tree line and to have penetrated the forested coast of central Labrador. How they lived in this sub-Arctic environment and the nature of their relationship with the Indians whose country it had been are mysteries that archaeology has yet to unravel.

Their contacts with local Indian groups, however, may have had one consequence of great significance for later history: the introduction of the bow and arrow to the Indian peoples of the New World. Small stone weapon points, which appear to be copies of Palaeo-Eskimo arrowheads, are found on Indian settlement sites in the area occupied about 2000 BC, shortly after the Palaeo-Eskimos arrived. The earliest stone arrowheads on archaeological sites in other regions of the New World appear at progressively later times as one moves farther south and west from Labrador. The Palaeo-Eskimos, therefore, may have been instrumental in introducing an element of Old World technology that became the prime weapon of most New World peoples.

The continued contacts between peoples with such different backgrounds as the Palaeo-Eskimos and the Indians of the Labrador coast must have resulted in other transfers of technology, ideas, and beliefs. Some of the ideas picked up by the newcomers to the area may have helped shape the distinctive direction that later Palaeo-Eskimo culture developed in the eastern Arctic.

Greenland

Another resource-rich frontier was open to the coastal hunting Palaeo-Eskimo groups of the eastern Arctic: the large island, or semi-continent, of Greenland. The route to this new land must have begun on the mountainous northern coast of Baffin Island, where Palaeo-Eskimos, like the local Inuit of today, hunted migrating sea mammals as they moved along the narrow leads of Lancaster Sound. The loom of another mountainous and ice-capped land to the north must have tempted explorers, and a quick reconnaissance made over stable spring ice may have returned with news of a coast occupied only by caribou, muskoxen, and the sea mammals that thronged the widening ice leads of early summer. The eventual settlement of the new land, what we now know as Devon Island, may have waited until the Baffin Islanders were troubled by social problems in the local community, or perhaps by an outbreak of sickness, or heavy ice conditions that prevented an anticipated and necessary spring hunt.

Social problems motivated a similar event among the northern Baffin Inuit of the 1860s, propelling a small group of families across the ice of Lancaster Sound to try their luck in the unoccupied lands to the north. Over a period of three years this group moved along the steep and glacier-strewn coasts of eastern Devon and Ellesmere islands, and eventually settled in the Thule district of northwestern Greenland. Similar migrations into unoccupied countries, perhaps precipitated by similar problems, are easily imagined for the early Palaeo-Eskimo peoples. The nineteenth-century Inuit example also provides a time scale by which to measure such events – in this case a displacement of approximately 700 kilometres in a three-year period – and suggests a model that may have contributed to the apparently rapid dispersion of Palaeo-Eskimo bands across Arctic North America.

When early Palaeo-Eskimo migrants reached the area where northwestern Greenland and Ellesmere Island are separated only by the narrows of Smith Sound, they would have been faced by two choices. To the north lay the broad polar deserts of Pearyland and northern Ellesmere Island, populated by herds of muskoxen, caribou, and arctic hares. To the southeast stretched the frightening coastline of Melville Bay, where the ice cap of the Greenland interior fronts directly on a frozen ocean. The people who chose each of the two routes to new land developed distinctly different ways of life, but there are enough similarities in the artifacts left behind to suggest that they shared a common ancestry in the remote past.

Those who chose the northern lands evolved the very distinctive Independence culture described in the previous chapter, an adaptation to the land mammal resources and vast seasonal differences of the extreme High Arctic. Those who braved the ice front of Melville Bay discovered a much richer land to the south, on the mountainous islands and deep fiords of the west Greenland coast. Here they evolved the way of life known to archaeologists as the Saqqaq culture. Living in a region where the sea mammal resources of the coasts fronting Baffin Bay were balanced by the caribou herds of the inner fiords, they evolved an adaptation generally similar to that of their relatives who occupied the coastal regions of Baffin Island, northern Hudson Bay, and Labrador. As in those areas, the settlements occupied by the Saqqaq people seem to have been large and continuously occupied over periods of several centuries.

The west coast of Greenland must have been another major centre of Palaeo-Eskimo cultural development, although isolated from the broad expanse of Palaeo-Eskimo settlement across Davis Strait in the Canadian Arctic. The Saqqaq people thrived for over 1,000 years in a rich and productive environment. But when environmental conditions began to change in Arctic North America, and various groups of Palaeo-Eskimos were forced to adapt their way of life to the new conditions, the isolation of the Saqqaq people may have proved their eventual downfall.

New Homelands

By approximately 2000 BC, most regions of the New World Arctic were home to small and scattered bands of Palaeo-Eskimos. During the previous centuries, these people had accomplished the last major land-taking of an unoccupied region of the earth. They had explored countries that had been beyond the bounds of human knowledge and experience, had learned their secrets, and with a simple technology but a great deal of knowledge and adaptability, had learned to live and flourish in the new lands.

We have imagined this accomplishment as if it had involved only a half-dozen steps across the boundaries between different environmental regions. This is, of course, a vast simplification of the process as it must have really happened. For centuries, hundreds of individual families made lifetimes of decisions about where to spend the coming winter, or where the best prospects lay for a summer hunt, or whether a move was necessary in order to escape a feud, illness, or poor hunting. As the geography and environment of Arctic North America became gradually incorporated into the knowledge, mythology, and beliefs of the Palaeo-Eskimo immigrants, they absorbed the new country as much as it absorbed them. After a few centuries in their new homelands, memories of their ancestors' early wanderings must have vanished from all but the vaguest of their traditional stories. They were now a part of the country, as much at home in their own lands as were any nations on earth.

The Palaeo-Eskimos differed from most other nations, however, in the isolation that they enjoyed. Aside from wary contacts with the Indian groups of the neighbouring forests and with the changing populations of the Bering Sea region, they remained quarantined for approximately 3,000 years from the technological, social, and cultural changes occurring in more temperate regions of the world. That vast span of time in isolation, combined with the extreme nature of their adaptation to the harshest environment on earth, was to produce a unique and fascinating human culture and way of life.

CHAPTER 6

When the Climate Changes

Climates are not supposed to change. Our society, like all others before it, has learned to accept the variable weather that is part of our local environments, but our economy and way of life are not adapted to anything beyond a certain range of tolerable variation. When we are threatened by more major changes, on a scale that would turn wheatlands into deserts or raise ocean levels as the polar icecaps melt, we become rightfully concerned that our way of life will be irrevocably altered.

Our society is not the first to face the threat of a major shift in global climates. The past decades have seen remarkable advances in scientific techniques to recover evidence of early environmental changes. These techniques have shown that changes on the scale of that predicted for the coming century, or on an even more drastic scale, have taken place at irregular intervals throughout human history. The causes are not nearly as clear as the events themselves; variations in solar radiation, in the concentration of atmospheric carbon dioxide, in atmospheric circulation patterns, or in the transfer of heat by major ocean currents have all been proposed by some scientists and rejected by the majority of others.

How Climates Change

Very recent scientific work has produced startling findings on the speed of past climatic changes. Deep cores drilled into the Greenland ice cap have penetrated thousands of years of accumulated ice, banded with annual layers much like tree rings. Each of these layers can be analyzed to provide information on such things as surface temperature at the time that the ice was formed, the amount of carbon dioxide in the air, and traces of chemicals and dusts in the atmosphere. These studies have now shown that events as significant as the end of the last Ice Age occurred over only a few years each, and perhaps in single years. Scientists had presumed that such major climatic events were long and gradual processes, occurring over centuries or millennia. If global climatic change can occur practically instantaneously – if an ice age begins in one year when summer doesn't arrive across the polar and temperate world – then speculation on the causes of climatic change and on how human societies react must be drastically revised. In the search for the causes of climatic change, the betting now seems to be on changes in major deep-ocean currents as the triggering device for sudden shifts in global climate.

While climatologists and other scientists were demonstrating that climate was not a particularly stable phenomenon, archaeologists and historians began to speculate on the links between climatic change and many of the events and developments in human history. These theories found especially fertile ground when applied to the histories of Arctic peoples. Arctic climates are so severe, and human adaptations to them are assumed to be so marginal, that any significant change in the environment could be expected to cause major problems for the people adapted to it. In addition, traditional Arctic peoples had so little technological insulation between themselves and their environment that an unexpected change must have forced on them a simple choice between swift adaptation or death by cold and starvation. Unlike in today's world, famine could not be alleviated by large-scale storage or by importing huge cargoes of food from another continent. The new evidence of rapid climatic change indicates that people would have had to undertake drastic adaptation to new conditions on a scale of months rather than years or decades.

Did the climatic history of the Arctic regions play a major role in the history of the Palaeo-Eskimos? By combining archaeological evidence with that from the study of ice cores, tree rings, fossil pollen, and other techniques for investigating ancient climates, we may gain some insight into changes during the three thousand years or more that the Palaeo-Eskimos occupied Arctic North America.

The Postglacial Warm Period
The last Ice Age came to an end about 11,000 years ago. The climate of the Arctic suddenly warmed, soon reaching mean annual temperatures a few

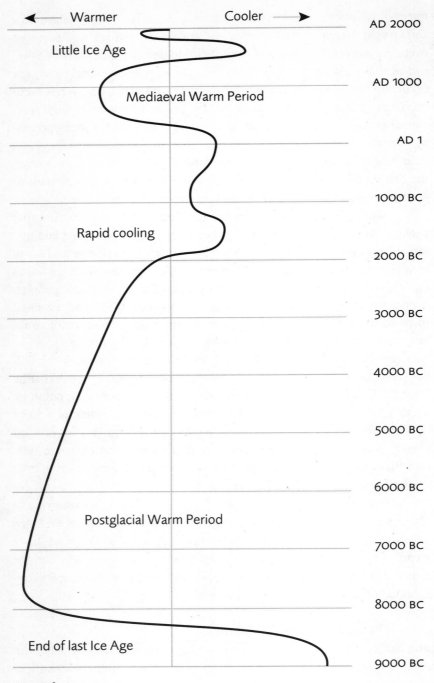

← Warmer   Cooler →

Little Ice Age

Mediaeval Warm Period

Rapid cooling

Postglacial Warm Period

End of last Ice Age

AD 2000

AD 1000

AD 1

1000 BC

2000 BC

3000 BC

4000 BC

5000 BC

6000 BC

7000 BC

8000 BC

9000 BC

FIGURE 6.1
Climatic change in Arctic Canada since the
last Ice Age

∧ The small spruce trees growing at the edge of the tundra are especially susceptible to cold weather. Variations in the width of growth rings record changes in past climates of the Arctic regions.

> Scientists remove a drill core from the Penny Ice Cap on Baffin Island. The layers in the ice contain a record of past Arctic climate.

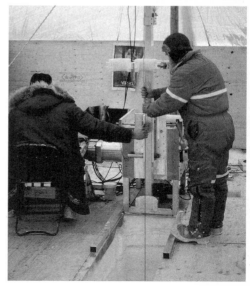

degrees warmer than those of today. The ice sheets that covered much of Arctic North America began to thaw and retreat, and the sea invaded channels freed from the melting ice. Whales were navigating the straits of the Arctic Archipelago by at least 8,000 years ago, and by 7,000 years ago waterfowl were nesting on the most northerly islands. The tree line advanced well to the north of its present position, and in more northerly regions the warm summers probably produced a relatively luxuriant tundra vegetation. This may in turn have supported significantly larger populations of caribou and muskoxen than those roaming today's Arctic. Sea ice was probably less extensive and lasted for a shorter season than it does at present.

The Postglacial Warm Period lasted for several thousands of years but was ending when the Palaeo-Eskimos began to expand across Arctic North America. By about 2500 BC the first Palaeo-Eskimo immigrants probably found a country in which the normal weather conditions were similar to those that now occur only in particularly warm and pleasant seasons. The difference would have been most noticeable in summer, when the snow quickly melted from the landscape, sea ice disappeared early in the season, and warm, storm-free days favoured autumn hunters. The relatively ice-free channels between Arctic islands served as a barrier to summer travel but distributed greater numbers of valuable driftwood logs than are found on modern beaches in the area. Winters may have been somewhat less stormy than at present but just as dark, and the cold must have been just as brutal.

These conditions, which we would probably consider exceptionally good if we were to visit the Arctic of 4,000 years ago, must have been considered normal by the Palaeo-Eskimos who encountered them for the first time. These were the conditions that they expected in the coming year and on which they based their calculations for coping with the economic necessities of the year. In a landscape where survival depends on correctly predicting the locations and availability of animals at various seasons, stable climatic and environmental conditions are extremely important. For the first few centuries of their occupation, the Palaeo-Eskimos seem to have found such stability across Arctic North America.

The First Chill
The first indications that the environment was not as stable as had been assumed must have come in the centuries between 2200 and 1500 BC.

Across the world, people were coping with situations beyond their experience and beyond the knowledge of traditions developed during the long Postglacial Warm Period. In Egypt, the Old Kingdom society of pyramid builders disintegrated in famine and civil war as the annual Nile floods failed to appear and the desert sands encroached. The great Harappan cities of the Indus valley were abandoned and destroyed as changes in circulation patterns diverted the expected monsoon rains.

By this time the Palaeo-Eskimos had occupied most Arctic regions for several centuries and had developed economies that were closely attuned to the local conditions. When the climate began to change, each region of the Arctic must have been touched in a different way, and the effects of the changes were felt at different times. Accordingly, adaptation was not a uniform process but a matter of individual bands accommodating their way of life to local environments that were no longer behaving as expected. What we can detect archaeologically is a general picture that reflects numerous individual decisions and their consequences.

The Independence culture muskox-hunters of the extreme High Arctic may have been among the first to be affected by the new conditions. Very few archaeological sites in the area seem to have been occupied after about 1500 BC. Entire regions may have been abandoned as cooler summers prevented the already sparse tundra vegetation from replenishing itself after animal grazing and as muskox populations rapidly declined or disappeared. Local hunting bands dependent on these animals must have either died of starvation or joined other groups where muskoxen still thrived. Eventually only a few bands – located in areas where conditions continued to sustain both animal and human populations – may have survived to maintain the cultural traditions of the Independence people.

The situation may have been similar in more southerly regions, where there is an apparent decline in occupations of the eastern Canadian Arctic over this period. These groups must have depended on sea mammals for a major portion of their food supply, and they may have been especially vulnerable to unexpected changes in sea ice conditions and the availability of sea animals. If a band organized their winter food supply to last until migrating seals appeared in opening ice leads the following May and the leads did not open until June as a result of cold weather and

For Arctic hunters, the most significant effect of climatic change was the variation it produced in the extent and seasonal duration of sea ice. The unexpected appearance of open water could be just as disastrous as unusually early or extensive ice.

winds from an unusual direction, no one might survive to see the arrival of the first seals. As in the extreme High Arctic, human groups on the eastern Arctic islands may have persisted only in localities that were buffered from the worst of the changes inflicted on the environment.

In contrast, Palaeo-Eskimos continued to thrive on Victoria and Banks islands in the central Arctic and in the adjacent mainland region of the Barren Grounds. The environmental changes that occurred elsewhere after 2000 BC, and that may have chilled the previously warm climate only to conditions similar to those of today, do not seem to have had a negative impact on human adaptation to these more continental regions. Perhaps the changes in circulation that brought cooler weather to the eastern Arctic did not yet affect the regions to the west. For several more centuries, these areas may have enjoyed temperature and moisture regimes that promoted abundant vegetation and supported dense populations of caribou and muskoxen. Archaeological sites occupied after 1500 BC indicate that land mammal populations were sufficiently large for the Palaeo-Eskimo bands of the central Arctic to make major kills.

One of the most impressive sites dating to this period is named Umingmak – the word for muskox in Inuttituut – and lies on a small knoll in the prairie-like interior of Banks Island. Scattered down the slopes of the hill are the bones of several hundred muskoxen, mixed with the chipped-stone tools and other artifacts left by the Palaeo-Eskimo hunters who killed the animals. Well over a hundred muskox skulls are buried in the turf, many of them placed in a line to form a wall or windbreak; such heavy and unwieldy bones are rarely carried from a distant kill, and their presence suggests that many of the muskoxen were hunted very close to the site. The abundance of bones, and the evidence they provide for nearby hunting, suggests that Banks Island must have supported a very dense muskox population, as it does today, and that a band of Palaeo-Eskimos made a very productive living in the area over a period of several generations.

An even larger set of sites has been excavated from the shores of the Ekalluk River in southern Victoria Island. This area forms a natural trap for migrating caribou, which are funnelled into a narrow gap between the coast and a very long lake. The trap has been improved by the construction of several kilometres of drive lanes, rows of piled boulders or vertically placed slabs that the caribou could mistake for hunters and that would thus channel the herds toward an ambush. These drive lanes were still being used by Inuit hunters of the present century, and it seems likely that they were first built by the Palaeo-Eskimos, whose tools have been found among the slaughtered remains of hundreds of caribou, and then set up repeatedly over generations of continuous occupancy. The stone tools found at these sites are very similar to those from the Umingmak site on adjacent Banks Island, and the sites seem to have been occupied at about the same time.

New Territories

These successful predators of caribou and muskoxen did not restrict their hunting to the islands of the central Arctic. Sites with similar styles of stone tools begin to appear across the caribou lands of the Barren Grounds at the same period and are even found hundreds of kilometres south of the present tree line. There is no evidence that Indian groups occupied the northern forest regions during these centuries of Palaeo-Eskimo habitation, as they had at earlier times and as they did during the past several hundred years.

The withdrawal of Indian groups from the northern portions of their forest homelands and their replacement by Palaeo-Eskimos coincided with a southward shift of the tree line to somewhere close to its present position. This change in the Barren Grounds environment was probably accompanied by massive disruption in the migration patterns of the region's caribou herds, and consequently of the human groups that were so closely tied to their movements. The stumps of ancient trees, which can still be found far north of today's tree line, are often charred and suggest that the forest retreat occurred through a series of widespread forest fires. Perhaps the trees of the far northern forest were put under stress by cold weather, made susceptible to insect damage, and the dying forests became vulnerable to extensive fires. Widespread burning episodes would be very effective in diverting the movements of migrating caribou and would be disastrous to people whose livelihood was based on predicting those movements. Under conditions such as this we can easily imagine the extinction of local forest hunting bands and their replacement by Palaeo-Eskimo bands moving south into the tundra-like environment of the devastated forests. Whatever the sequence of events, archaeological sites prove that Palaeo-Eskimos were living and hunting in interior regions as far south as Lake Athabaska, and that this southward expansion lasted for several centuries before the northern forests were reclaimed by Dene Indian groups.

Cold Weather and Good Hunting

The cooler conditions that set in after 2000 BC lasted for about a millennium, and then the Arctic climate took another step into the cold. The centuries between 1000 BC and AD 1 saw colder conditions around the northern hemisphere, and these may have been especially marked in Arctic regions. The onset of significantly colder climates may have been disastrous to some groups. The Palaeo-Eskimo occupation of southern Greenland disappeared at this time, perhaps because no groups adapted rapidly enough to changes in local environments. Greenland's isolation from the rest of the Arctic is reflected in the fact that its southern coasts remained uninhabited for almost 1,000 years.

A similar local extinction may have occurred along the coast of Labrador, which has a very similar environment to that of southern Greenland, and perhaps in other regions of Arctic Canada. In all these areas, however, the earlier occupants seem to have been soon replaced by newer Palaeo-Eskimo groups who shared a novel and different set of artifacts. The new technology was probably associated with new knowledge and abilities in coping with environmental conditions unknown to their ancestors. With this new set of capabilities, the Palaeo-Eskimos soon demonstrated that a colder climate did not necessarily produce a poorer environment for Arctic hunters. Their dwelling sites soon became larger and more permanent than any known from earlier periods. In many areas, people began building permanent winter houses from boulders and turf and heating them with soapstone lamps that burned sea mammal oil. The artifacts recovered from such sites are more diverse than those from earlier Palaeo-Eskimo settlements, and among them are found increasing numbers of small carvings and other objects showing artistic enthusiasm and accomplishment.

These later Palaeo-Eskimo settlements are referred to as the Dorset culture. As archaeologists began to examine the artifacts recovered from these sites, it became apparent that they belonged to the cultural tradition that had been named in 1925 by Diamond Jenness on the basis of a collection of artifacts he had received from near Cape Dorset on Baffin

Island. Jenness was finally proven correct in his assumption that these artifacts represented a way of life considerably older than that of the Inuit occupants of Arctic Canada.

Dorset culture artifacts obviously reflect a richer and more secure way of life than that of earlier Palaeo-Eskimos. The change seems to relate to the Dorset people's ability and efficiency in hunting sea mammals: seal, walrus, beluga, and narwhal. The largest and most enduring Dorset settlements are found in areas where sea mammals are abundant today, and there is little evidence of Dorset occupation in interior regions.

The Dorset people apparently thrived during a period when the climate was rapidly cooling, eventually reaching conditions that were significantly colder than those of today. Their success under such conditions appears to contradict our almost automatic assumption that economic opportunities in the Arctic should decline during a period of colder climate. This probably holds true for people whose adaptations resemble those of the traditional Inuit, whose most productive economic activities were divided between interior hunting of caribou and maritime hunting of sea mammals during the summer season of open water. For such people, a cooling climate would signify decreased caribou populations and less accessible sea mammals because of a diminished season and extent of open water. But the opposite might be the case for the Dorset culture Palaeo-Eskimos, who appear to have abandoned the bow as a hunting weapon and who lacked the sophisticated boats and open-water hunting gear of the Inuit. In most regions of the Arctic, Dorset hunting appears to have been based on taking sea mammals from shore or from the sea ice. For such hunters, more extensive sea ice and a longer season during which this hunting platform was available may well have produced a much more efficient and productive economy than that practised by their ancestors.

Sea ice environments, and especially ice-edge environments, are much more productive than the open ocean. The bottom of the ice is an inverted landscape on which innumerable plankton and other small creatures graze. The chilled, oxygen-rich and food-dense water serves as a feeding ground for fish, and they in turn attract seals and whales, which congregate about the edges of the ice. Walrus use sea ice as a home, from which they dive to feed on the shellfish beds associated with such waters. Expanses of stable ice provide shelter for ringed and bearded seals, which maintain breathing holes throughout the winter and whelp in snow dens on the spring ice. In waters farther south, the spring pack ice that flows down the coasts of Labrador and Newfoundland provides a nursery for vast herds of harp and hooded seals.

The Dorset people seem to have mastered hunting these animals, becoming in their turn an ice-adapted species. The colder conditions of the first millennium BC allowed them to expand this way of life throughout the central and eastern Arctic, including the eventual reoccupation of Greenland. They also moved into more southerly coastal regions, becoming efficient predators of whelping seal herds off the coasts of Labrador and the Gulf of St. Lawrence. To the Dorset people, the white-coated seal pups scattered over hundreds of square kilometres of ice may have been the key that allowed them to expand their way of life into the sub-Arctic regions of Atlantic Canada.

A Global Warming

The transition to an ice-hunting economy allowed the Dorset people not only to expand their territory but to achieve a stable adaptation that was to support their way of life for 1,500 years. When Dorset occupations eventually began to disappear from one region after another the climate was once again changing, and it seems plausible that the two events may have been linked. In this case, the northern hemisphere was becoming warmer. For an ice-adapted people such as the Dorsets, a warming climate and less extensive sea ice may have proved more distressing than the colder conditions of earlier times.

Throughout the three millennia during which the Palaeo-Eskimos were the primary occupants of Arctic Canada and Greenland, the effect of changing climate on the people and their way of life provides an instructive example of how humans react to weather patterns that fall outside the range a society considers normal and expected. In the early centuries of Palaeo-Eskimo occupation, a cooling climate forced the abandonment of some regions but opened others to occupation. Then a much colder climate saw the development of the Dorset culture and economy, which seems to have used the change as an opportunity to expand population, territory, and economic security. Finally, the warming conditions of the first millennium AD are both directly and indirectly associated with the end of the Palaeo-Eskimo way of life, for the open-water conditions not only brought starvation but also attracted an invasion from the Alaskan Inuit.

The links between climate and human welfare may be especially close and clearly visible in Arctic regions. Yet the climatic changes that affected the Palaeo-Eskimos are also associated, although more obscurely, with major changes in human societies living in more temperate regions of the world. Our own economy and society is perhaps more closely tied to expected weather conditions than we seem to think. In a period when imminent climatic change is predicted and expected, we might be wise to re-examine the links between our own way of life and the environment on which it is based. We may not be as vulnerable as the Palaeo-Eskimos, but we will probably be as surprised and unprepared as they were by sudden shifts in weather patterns, and our reactions to these shifts will probably be just as fraught with risk.

CHAPTER 7

How an Arctic Culture Was Transformed

The Palaeo-Eskimo cultural tradition was led in a slow and stately dance with a climate that followed unheard and unpredictable music. For 3,000 years the dance continued, each step in a changing climate followed by a shift in the ways in which local Palaeo-Eskimo groups lived and coped with their environment.

One of the most striking measures in this dance occurred with the onset of colder climatic conditions in the centuries around 500 BC. As we have seen, the Palaeo-Eskimo occupants of the eastern Arctic met the challenge by developing new tools and weapons and changing their living patterns. Archaeologists refer to these changes as the development of the Dorset culture. Contrary to what might be expected in a cooling Arctic environment, the Dorset people expanded their population and developed a richer and more secure way of life than that existing previously. The present chapter attempts to understand this unanticipated and propitious development.

How Does 'Adaptation' Really Work?

To say that the Arctic climate led Palaeo-Eskimo culture in a dance offers an evocative image but doesn't pretend to explain how cultural changes developed in response to changes in environments. When we wish to explain these processes we usually talk in terms of 'adaptation.' In this case we speculated that cooling climates increased the extent and seasonal duration of sea ice in the gulfs and channels of the Canadian Arctic, thus expanding the opportunities for sea mammal hunters who sought their prey from the ice edge. These people responded to new conditions by inventing new sets of artifacts and developing new spheres of knowledge regarding ice and the animals associated with ice.

Such a set of speculations may sound more reasonable than the analogy of a dance, but it tells us little more about actual events over the few generations that established the Dorset way of life. Both the dance image and the adaptation story are abstractions from human experience. They attempt to comprehend a large-scale process and its long-term results. They cannot discern events on the scale of individual lives and individual families faced with unexpected and dangerous situations. Yet what we so facilely term the development of Dorset culture is nothing but the sum of hundreds or thousands of such events.

We have only three tools to help us penetrate to this level of ancient reality. The first of these is archaeological evidence, which is scarce, interpreted with difficulty, and relates directly to only a few scattered episodes in the huge geographical and temporal range of Palaeo-Eskimo life. Our second tool is the knowledge of how other peoples, particularly the Inuit who occupied these areas over the past centuries, have coped with similar environments. Finally, we have our imaginations to assemble these two types of evidence into a picture, which must in some ways have resembled traditional Inuit life but in others have been markedly different.

Palaeo-Eskimo Society

Before asking how social and cultural change occurred in Palaeo-Eskimo society, we should try to understand the society itself. The most promising starting point in our search is the related societies of the Inuit. The Inuit of Arctic Canada and Greenland traditionally grouped themselves into a large number of distinct local societies, or bands. Each of these bands was named after a locality or a feature of its homeland, with the name ending in the suffix -miut, meaning 'the people of.' The group occupying the Kent Peninsula area of the central Arctic, for example, were known to themselves and their neighbours as the Umingmaktormiut, 'the people of the muskox'; the group whose activities focused on the Fury and Hecla Strait area at the north end of Melville Peninsula were known as the Iglulingmiut, 'the people who live where there are houses.'

A few of these groups had up to 500 or even 1,000 members, but the majority had barely more than 200 people. Each local Inuit band was distinguished from its neighbours by details of clothing style, the forms of its artifacts, and its dialect, although these details were often so minor that they would only be noticed by members of the bands themselves. To an individual, band society combined many of the characteristics that a contemporary urban person would attach to family, community, and nation. One grew up and was educated, made a living, found a marriage partner, and could expect to be cared for in old age within the same small society. Most or all of one's known relatives lived in the band, and members could expect to go through life only occasionally meeting humans who belonged to other bands.

Every band was divided into several extended family groups, each centred around one or two key individuals: the parents of several grown sons, the eldest of several brothers, or a person whose skill at hunting or magic or trading with other peoples provided support and protection for relatives. These large, family-based groups were the main economic units of the society. Each was economically self-sufficient and contained enough hunters to undertake communal hunting projects or to share food in times of scarcity. The members of extended families endeavoured to live in one place and to hunt and work together whenever local food resources would allow. When food was scarce or animals were more widely scattered, groups broke into individual families composed of husband and wife, children, and perhaps a grandparent, another dependent relative, or an orphaned child. These small groups were perfectly capable of living on their own, a capability that allowed the Inuit to take best advantage of their huge territory and reduced the risk of starvation for all.

The members of a band came together rarely. Such assemblies usually occurred only annually or semi-annually and were timed to coincide with a concentration of food resources that would support the entire group. These occasions were marked by feasting, dancing, games, gossip, and the pairing of marriage partners. They were times for renewing old friendships, establishing new partnerships and alliances, comparing or trading tools and hunting equipment made over the past months, and admiring the new clothing that had been prepared for the festival. These were exciting times, especially for the young people, and they were made to last as long as possible. Eventually, however, economic necessity or social impulses led individual families or extended family groups back to their traditional living areas, and the band as a unit ceased to function for another few months.

The extreme flexibility of such a social organization seems admirably suited to both human social needs and the economic conditions of the Arctic environment. We can probably assume that other hunting peoples living in this environment in the past must have organized themselves in much the same way, although the details of group size and inter-family partnerships may have differed. The basic organization of Inuit society serves as the best available model on which to reconstruct the social organization of the Palaeo-Eskimos.

Nevertheless, we must take into account that Palaeo-Eskimo techniques of hunting and travelling would have been considerably less efficient than those of the Inuit. This probably resulted in lower population densities in most Arctic regions: the total Palaeo-Eskimo population is likely to have been significantly smaller than the Inuit population and the people more widely scattered across the landscape. This in turn must have been reflected in social organization. As in Inuit times, local Palaeo-Eskimo societies would have required at least 200 people to maintain themselves as biological units within which most marriages occurred. The territories occupied by these units must have been considerably larger though, and there were probably few societies with populations much larger than 200 or 300 people. Ernest S. Burch, the eminent anthropologist and historian on whose work the above description of Inuit societies draws heavily, estimates that in AD 1800 there may have been fifty Inuit bands between the Mackenzie River and the Atlantic coast. On the other hand, in 1800 BC or 800 BC only ten or twenty Palaeo-Eskimo groups may have occupied the same area.

Within the local band, the technologies and hunting abilities of the Palaeo-Eskimos may not have been capable of supporting large, extended-family camp groups for more than limited periods. Instead, individual families could have been forced to live as isolated units for a greater portion of the year than was the case for many Inuit groups. This seems to coincide with the archaeological evidence, especially that relating to the early Palaeo-Eskimo occupations, prior to the development of Dorset culture. Many early Palaeo-Eskimo sites are composed of either single dwellings or small clusters of two or three dwellings, which may not have been occupied simultaneously. Most larger sites appear to have been inhabited for only brief periods.

This atomization of the community – in which local societies

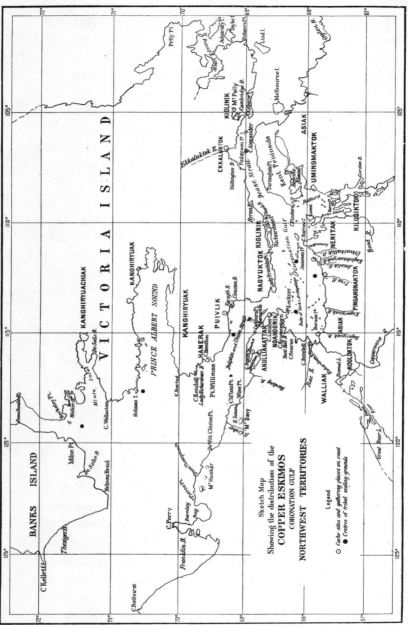

MAP 7.1

Distribution of Copper Inuit bands according to Diamond Jenness, 1915. Each band occupies a named territory in the Victoria Island-Coronation Gulf area. The Palaeo-Eskimo world must have been similarly divided into named band territories.

Source: Diamond Jenness, The Life of the Copper Eskimos. Report of the Canadian Arctic Expedition, 1913-18, vol. 12A (Ottawa: Government of Canada 1922)

functioned as units for only a few days per year and much of the year was spent in individual family units dispersed across a vast countryside – must have been especially marked in times of climatic and environmental stress. It was at such a time, and in the context of such a social organization, that we must attempt to imagine the changes that were to lead to the Dorset culture and way of life.

Family Tragedies and Cultural Change

The centuries between about 1500 and 1000 BC span a gap in our archaeological knowledge of Arctic North America. Very few sites are known to date from this period, and we suspect that these centuries saw a decline in Palaeo-Eskimo populations across the north. Some regions seem to have been abandoned, while in others the size of the local population may have been so diminished that their archaeological remains are not apparent. When archaeological sites reappear after this interval, the tools and weapons lost or abandoned around the dwellings are made in quite different styles from those known in earlier times. More interestingly, the new styles are relatively uniform wherever they appear, from Labrador to Hudson Bay and far northern Greenland. Together, these shifts mark the first phase in the development of a new Palaeo-Eskimo way of life.

What transformations can we imagine having occurred in Palaeo-Eskimo society to produce the types of changes that we see in the archaeological record? If we begin with the environmental context of the period, we see a time of climatic cooling and probably of climatic instability. The environment was not behaving as expected, and people found it increasingly difficult to predict the sea ice conditions or movements of animals on which their hunting depended. These conditions did not affect every Arctic region at the same time or with equal severity, so a wide range of responses must have occurred.

The most basic and probably the most common catalyst in bringing about change was a family disaster. Most such events would have occurred during the winter season, when the population was at its most dispersed, isolated, and vulnerable. We can imagine any number of occurrences precipitating tragedy: a heavy fall of early winter snow and freezing rain starved the muskoxen and hid the caches of meat accumulated during the fall; early autumn sea ice allowed the caribou to migrate south before an adequate fall hunt had been made; seals disappeared from local channels when sea ice did not melt during a short summer; or a hunter became ill, broke a leg on slippery rocks, or perished in an unexpected early blizzard. In the accumulation of such simple and poignant events, we may discover the explanation for the types of change that archaeology records.

The multiplication of family-level tragedies during a period of severe environmental conditions must have produced changes at the band level of Palaeo-Eskimo social organization. In some regions, the few families arriving at the fishing river or nesting cliff that provided sustenance for a spring assembly may have found themselves alone, the sole survivors of a hard and hungry winter that had massacred the other members of their society. Other band assemblies may have been better attended but heard tales of strangers who had been driven from their own lands by starvation and were searching for survival in the territories of other bands. Others may have listened to the reports of travellers who had gone in search of trade and found only empty and uninhabited lands where neighbouring peoples had once lived.

In most of the small and scattered communities celebrating their brief annual opportunity to spend time with distant relatives and friends, the talk must have been of hard times, scarce animals, and poor weather. There must have also been discussions about how local bands should cope with the situation and how life could be made more secure during the coming winter. Families that had barely survived until spring might decide to try their fortune in another part of the territory, combining their efforts and luck with people more fortunate. Others might decide to attempt a wintering in a region whose original occupants had disappeared, in the hope of finding more animals than in their own home area.

For bands that had been decimated by poor hunting and bad luck, more drastic solutions were necessary. If the animals on which their lives depended had abandoned their territory, the people must follow. Such a decision would involve depending on very distant relatives or mere acquaintances in order to gain acceptance in a neighbouring territory. A band that had been reduced to only a few families could not provide the safety, marriage partners, and social support necessary for long-term survival. Situations such as this must have been the major stimulus to the movement of families into new, long-abandoned, or alien territories. The general decrease in population that attended a deteriorating environment

This photograph depicts a spring gathering of an early twentieth-century Inuit band. From a distance, a band gathering of Palaeo-Eskimo peoples must have looked much like this.

must inevitably have increased movement, interaction, and communication among the various isolated Palaeo-Eskimo populations of Arctic Canada and Greenland. Such an enforced mobility over relatively long distances and across what had previously been cultural boundaries between neighbouring bands might be expected to produce the characteristics that appear on archaeological sites dating to the centuries after 1000 BC.

The Archaeology of a Changing Culture

The Rivendell site mentioned in Chapter 4 was occupied toward the end of the period of apparently low population density between about 1500 and 1000 BC, and the artifacts recovered from this small camp show the earliest clear evidence that the Independence people of northern Ellesmere Island were in contact with Palaeo-Eskimo populations occupying more southerly regions. This evidence appears in the form of artifact styles and types with an obvious resemblance to those in use in other Arctic regions: a small lamp carved from soft stone is similar to those used by the Saqqaq people of southwestern Greenland; bone lance heads with slits along the edges for sharp stone blades resemble ones from the earliest Dorset settlements, near Igloolik in the central Arctic; needles with flattened cross-sections instead of the circular cross-sections of earlier Palaeo-Eskimo needles are precursors of forms found throughout Arctic Canada in the following centuries.

The few new artifact types do not suggest that the Rivendell people were newcomers from some other Arctic region. Most of their tools are similar to those used by earlier inhabitants of the area, and their interior-oriented economic adaptation – based on the hunting of muskoxen – suggests continuities in local occupation. The evidence does, however, suggest that the Palaeo-Eskimo band whose territory encompassed northern Ellesmere Island no longer lived in total isolation. We might imagine that they learned of stone lamps from the discovery of a starvation camp, where a family of Greenlandic people had perished while searching for animals in a territory beyond their homeland. The remnants of a band of Ellesmere Islanders, wandering south in search of relief from starvation, may have encountered and traded with families who hunted seals rather than muskoxen. Perhaps the southern hunters copied the strong bone lances carried by the strangers from the north and the northern needleworkers were enthralled by the strong and sharp needles that their new acquaintances used. The new styles, which began as curiosities, may have been gradually adopted by neighbours and by the following generation to produce the change that we see in archaeological collections.

Similar events may be imagined across Arctic Canada during this time of hardship and wandering. Archaeological sites dating from the centuries after 1000 BC show similar mixtures of new and old artifact styles and an increasingly wide occurrence of certain styles previously confined to local regions. Flat needles with elongated eyes began to be used by all Palaeo-Eskimo groups. The chisel-like burins that were the primary bone-carving tools of early Palaeo-Eskimos were replaced by tools ground from hard flints and jades. Chipped-stone blades for knives and weapons began to be made with side notches, indicating a new technique for hafting the points to their bone handles or shafts. The same points began to be sharpened in a newly invented way, by a blow on the tip that removed a flat, wedge-shaped segment and formed a fresh edge (Plate 1).

Sites containing various combinations of these new artifacts and styles occur across the High Arctic, where archaeologists identify them as Independence II culture. Far to the south, remarkably similar collections are found in a series of settlements along the coast of Labrador and as far south as the island of Newfoundland; here they are called Groswater Dorset culture, named after Groswater Bay in central Labrador. The Groswater people were the first Palaeo-Eskimos to accomplish widespread settlement of coastal Newfoundland and to exploit the herds of whelping harp seals on the spring ice of the Gulf of St. Lawrence. Between these two widely separated regions, somewhat similar collections are known from both the southern and northeastern coasts of Baffin Island.

Our clearest view of this development comes from the series of raised beaches near Igloolik, in Fury and Hecla Strait between Baffin Island and the Arctic mainland. The earliest Palaeo-Eskimo settlements in this area date to perhaps 2500 BC and now lie at elevations almost fifty metres above present sea level, raised to this altitude by geological uplift of the local landscape. Subsequent settlements have not been lifted as high, and the long sequence of pre-Dorset camps lies on beaches from fifty to twenty-four metres above today's coast. The sequence is so continuous and change in artifact styles so gradual as one descends from one beach ridge to the next that we can imagine the area occupied continuously by the same band of people for 3,000 years or more. The changes that occurred elsewhere across the Arctic from 1000 to 500 BC appear in camps at elevations between twenty-four and twenty-two metres above present sea level, on beaches that would have formed the coastline just before 500 BC. Ground slate knives and carved soapstone lamps suddenly appear in the archaeological deposits; the bow and arrow seems to have been dropped from use in favour of the hand-held lance; new types of harpoons and fish spears materialize, as well as bone sled shoes, large knives for cutting snow blocks, and crampons for walking on ice. Artifact styles quickly changed to conform to the new fashions found across the eastern Arctic. The rate of cultural change at these elevations is so marked that Jorgen Meldgaard, the Danish archaeologist who excavated the Igloolik sites, sees this period as one of turmoil.

These centuries were obviously a time of transition for the peoples of Arctic Canada. The changing and unpredictable climate, the frequent episodes of hardship and starvation, and the spread of new artifacts and new ideas across vast areas of sparsely occupied land set the stage for a fundamental shift in the Palaeo-Eskimo economy and culture. The eventual product of this shift appears suddenly in the archaeological record, as the more settled and secure way of life that archaeologists term the Dorset culture.

Dorset Culture Emerges

The process of cultural and economic change culminated at some time around 500 BC. The archaeological evidence of a new way of life surfaces rather suddenly at this time, over an area extending from northern Labrador to Lancaster Sound and westward into the central Arctic. Throughout this vast area, people began to construct permanent winter villages at places where local hunting could support a sedentary existence throughout the coldest and darkest period of the year. These small clusters of houses are solid evidence for the development of a more comfortable and secure way of life. Only people who could accumulate enough food and fuel to last for weeks or months would be tempted to build such structures, and their very existence is a measure of the success of the Early Dorset people in adjusting to the colder climates of the period. As we speculated in the last chapter, the key to Dorset success probably lay in exploiting the sea ice environment, which became more extensive and longer lasting through the cold summers of the period.

Early Dorset winter houses were relatively large, rectangular structures, usually measuring roughly four by five metres. They were excavated into dry soil or gravel to a depth of up to fifty centimetres, to provide insulation and protection from the wind. The walls were built from the material dug from the house floor, supplemented by boulders and insulating blocks of turf. Roofs were probably covered with skins supported by driftwood poles, and the entire house heaped with snow for more insulation. The interior arrangement seems to have been based on the midpassage of earlier Palaeo-Eskimo dwellings, with a central alley paved and bordered by stone slabs, separating areas on either side of the house. Instead of the central hearth of earlier Palaeo-Eskimo tents, however, these houses were now heated by oil lamps carved from soapstone. Lamps provide a much more efficient source of heat and light than do open fires, and their smokeless flames can be used in a tightly closed and insulated dwelling.

The use of insulated houses heated by lamps also indicates that the occupants were efficient predators of sea mammals, on which they depended for the oil that was their new source of fuel. The bone middens surrounding Dorset villages provide further testimony to their hunting abilities. Instead of the thin scatter of caribou, muskox, seal, and bird bones strewn about early Palaeo-Eskimo tent camps, Dorset houses are often associated with thick piles of seal and walrus bones, as well as occasional bones of beluga and narwhal. The evidence is also much better preserved than on earlier sites, partially because the deeply dug houses and quickly accumulated middens provide better insulation for archaeological materials from the warmth and moisture of summer. The excellent preservation is probably also evidence of the colder climate of Early Dorset times, in which permafrost conditions invaded soil layers that would have thawed each summer during earlier centuries.

Because of the excellent preservation of its living sites, our archaeological picture of Dorset culture is more complete and more detailed than for earlier peoples. No longer must we strain our imaginations to piece together a way of life from a few stone tools and large mammal bones scattered around a boulder tent ring or an isolated hearth. Even in the more southerly regions of the Arctic, Dorset houses preserve a much

New kinds of artifacts were recovered
from the remains of Early Dorset houses,
among them lamps carved from soapstone,
ivory sled shoes, crampons for hunting
from smooth ice, and new and larger forms
of harpoons and lances.

The colder climatic conditions of the
Dorset period have resulted in improved
preservation of archaeological remains.
This thousand-year-old dwelling is covered
by a snowbank for all but a few days or
weeks each year, and the bedding material
of moss and heather is still preserved on
either side of the central passage.

wider range of materials: tools and weapons carved from bone and antler, stone blades mounted in wooden handles, tiny ivory carvings, occasional pieces of skin clothing, and even clippings of human hair. Our reconstruction of Dorset culture still relies heavily on the imagination, but it is supported by a much wider range of clues. A picture materializes of a way of life just as extraordinary as the one we have reconstructed for the early Palaeo-Eskimo ancestors of the Dorset people.

CHAPTER 8

The Dorset People

When the ancestors of the Inuit arrived in Arctic Canada from Alaska about 1,000 years ago, they discovered that the land was occupied by a strange people whom they called Tunit. Memories of the Tunit were preserved in the oral histories of the Inuit and passed down through more than thirty generations before being committed to writing during the present century. There seems to be little doubt that the Tunit of Inuit historians and the Dorset Palaeo-Eskimos of archaeologists (Plate 2) were one and the same. Traditional history converges with archaeology to provide a more complete picture of the Dorset people than we can paint of their remote Palaeo-Eskimo ancestors. The picture, however, is of a culture and a way of life that is not easy to understand from the perspective of either the traditional Inuit or the contemporary scientist.

The Tunit

'The *tunit* made our country habitable. They built the lines of boulder cairns that guide caribou to the river-crossings where they can be ambushed by hunters, and they furnished the rivers with fish-weirs.' The earliest occupants of Arctic Canada were thus depicted by an Inuk of the central Arctic Netsilingmiut people, whose historical knowledge was recorded in 1923. Inuit tradition portrayed the Tunit as a race of large people possessing great physical strength, who rejoiced in building with great boulders. The Iglulingmiut remembered them as superb hunters of walrus, who were so strong that they could break a walrus's neck with a harpoon line, and pull the huge animal home across the ice in the same way that an Inuk drags a seal. It was said that the Tunit loved their wives so much that when they saw the women waiting outside their houses they forgot their weariness and towed the walrus home with renewed vigour. Despite their strength, however, they were a timid and peaceable people; one Inuit historian noted that in the traditions with which he was familiar, 'nothing is told of their lust to kill.' This image of a strong and gentle people, great hunters and eager lovers, forms an attractive background against which we may try to interpret the archaeology of the Dorset culture.

Jade, Flint, and Quartz

Perhaps the most prosaic level of archaeological study, and the one most remote from the historical records of the Tunit, involves interpreting the small stone artifacts that served as the daily cutting tools for ancient peoples. These small utensils of chipped and polished stone must have been among the most common possessions of a Dorset man or woman. Yet a handful collected from the gravel surface of an ancient settlement or arranged in a museum cabinet can lead us along a path of exploration into the lives of the people who made and used such tools.

A collection of Dorset stone tools is unlike an assembly from any other time or cultural tradition. Many of the ideas that are fossilized in these tools can be traced back 4,000 years or more, to the earliest Palaeo-Eskimos and the artifacts that mark their arrival in the New World. We might imagine such ideas passed from one generation to the next as aesthetic instructions absorbed by each young craftsman from observing the work and products of his elders: stone tools should be small; a very specific type and quality of stone is appropriate for each kind of tool; strikingly coloured or patterned types of stone are superior to dull stones, even though they may be harder to find and to work with; and each kind of tool should be made to a precise pattern.

Along with aesthetic instructions from a cultural tradition, the Dorset stone worker knew that a specific kind of tool was required for each task. In some technological traditions, the same knife-like tool might be used for butchering an animal, scraping skins, cutting clothing patterns, carving a harpoon head from ivory, and forming a wooden harpoon shaft. For a Dorset craftsman, however, each task could best be carried out with a tool designed for that purpose alone. These traditional rules and practices resulted in brilliantly variegated sets of artifacts, tiny rainbows of

Dorset walrus hunters may have done most of their hunting from the ice edge, as did these Igloolik Inuit recorded during the explorer William Parry's expedition of 1822.

coloured and patterned stone that have been carefully chipped or polished to do a specific task.

In examining such a collection, archaeologists accustomed to dealing with the artifacts of other cultural traditions feel themselves in the presence of an unfamiliar and somewhat unsettling concept of technology. Moreau Maxwell, an American archaeologist who has devoted much of his life to understanding Dorset technology, reports that

> the cultural traces Dorset people have left behind have a fascinating, emotional effect on many of us ... To the archaeologist digging in the permafrost, where virtually everything is preserved, there is the frustrating feeling of being almost but not quite capable of understanding the totality of the material culture. Every artifact is made precisely, a point that increases our embarrassment in being unable to determine [its] function.

Everything is so small, so delicately and precisely formed, and so apparently inadequate to the tasks involved in making a living in an Arctic environment! The miniature scale of most Dorset tools suggests that they could have been made and used by human-like creatures only thirty centimetres tall. In fact, traditional Inuit stories about a diminutive race that lives beneath the ground seem to have been specifically associated with finds of Palaeo-Eskimo artifacts.

A set of Dorset stone tools inevitably suggests the metaphor of the Swiss Army knife. Both technologies arise from comparable traditions of ingenuity, miniaturization, and precise craftsmanship. Both combine many tiny and distinctive tools designed for specific purposes and capable of accomplishing a great deal of useful work with small hand movements. One of these familiar, red-handled, multipurpose artifacts would be the ideal gift for the first time traveller to present to a Dorset craftsperson.

The rules of Dorset craftsmanship also resulted in the development of extensive trade networks throughout the central and eastern Arctic. The aesthetics of tool making demanded the use of certain materials, and most of these occurred only in very restricted local areas. Dorset stoneworkers considered jade, for example, to be the appropriate material for making the polished, chisel-like tools for carving ivory and bone. Dorset prospectors located isolated deposits of jade and the closely related hard green rocks known as jadeite and nephrite in the Canadian Shield of the eastern Arctic. A local band with the good fortune to find jade

Dorset culture settlements were much larger and more permanent than those of their ancestors. This archaeological site, on the south coast of Devon Island, shows the remains of numerous Dorset structures, as well as some left by later Inuit occupants.

deposits within their territory could develop a profitable sideline in quarrying this rare material for trade with adjacent bands who lacked a source. Passing from hand to hand when neighbouring groups occasionally met and increasing in value with increasing distance from their source, small chunks of jade gradually penetrated every corner of the country occupied by Dorset people.

In a similar manner, many Dorset groups deemed crystalline quartz to be the most fitting material from which to make microblades, the tiny, razor-like flakes of stone that were the basic cutting tools of Dorset technology (Plate 3). Transparent as clear ice, growing from rough granite in perfectly hexagonal crystal columns, this unique substance was also traded widely throughout the Dorset world. Certain isolated quarries produced flint of a particular colour and pattern that was widely recognized as the best material from which to chip scraper blades or harpoon tips. Nuggets of pure copper were gathered from the rocks of the Coppermine River area in the central Arctic and traded as far as the most northerly Arctic islands. Iron was obtained from a cluster of huge meteorites that Dorset prospectors discovered near Cape York in far northwestern Greenland; small chunks of pure iron, chiselled from the meteorites and beaten to flat blades, were traded throughout Arctic Canada.

Each of these exotic substances had particular qualities that suited it to a specific use. These qualities, and the scarcity of the materials, must have endowed them with a high value in the eyes of Dorset craftsmen. Given other indications that magical and religious beliefs were important to Dorset culture people, we might expect magical qualities to be attributed to the small pieces of iron, copper, jade, and crystalline quartz that reached a Dorset band from distant and unknown lands. Magical traits may explain why certain scarce materials were traded and used over such wide areas, when local materials of apparently equal usefulness were available.

Most of the stone and metal tools made by Dorset craftsmen were so small that they could not be used directly in the hand. The Palaeo-Eskimo technological tradition had developed a set of techniques for hafting these tiny tools into a wide assortment of handles, each of which was again designed for a specific purpose. The permanently frozen middens of Dorset sites have provided us with occasional examples of these handles, showing a remarkable ingenuity in combining the functional qualities of materials such as bone, antler, ivory, small pieces of driftwood, sinew, and

Jade and blue-green slate provided attractive materials from which Dorset craftsmen ground and polished blades for tools.

blood-glue. Even hafted into usable handles, Dorset tools and utensils were small in comparison with those of most other cultural traditions. A Dorset family's knives, carving tools, scrapers, sewing equipment, soapstone lamps and pots, and other cooking utensils, would all fit easily into a small backpack. Armed with this portable toolkit, a family was furnished with all that they required to travel, to provide themselves with hunting weapons, to make new suits of clothing, to build a new house, and to establish themselves in a new location or a new country.

Lost Techniques

Considering the ingenuity and skill demonstrated by Dorset craftsmen, their artifacts show some very puzzling characteristics. Most striking, and almost the hallmark of Dorset technology, is the absence of drilled holes in any tools or weapons. The eyes of needles, the sockets of harpoon heads, and the small holes by which carved ivory amulets were suspended were all laboriously formed by gouging elongated grooves that eventually penetrated to the other side of the object.

Chipped-stone drill bits, mounted in wooden spindles and either twirled between the palms or spun with a bow drill, have been a staple of most technologies since the last Ice Age. The early Palaeo-Eskimo peoples of Arctic North America had used drills whenever their work required the perforation of a piece of bone or antler or ivory; even the tiny eyes of needles were pierced with tiny drill-bits. Given the efficiency of drilling as a method of working hard organic materials, and considering that earlier Palaeo-Eskimo peoples had long known the technique, why did Dorset craftsmen abandon their drills in favour of a much less efficient manufacturing method? Archaeologists have not been able to suggest a functional reason for the change.

The use of drills seems to have disappeared rather suddenly in the initial phases of Dorset culture development, at the same time that new styles of artifacts were being adopted throughout the Dorset world. If we cannot propose a functional reason why drills were forsaken, we might suggest that the technological change may have been accompanied by changes in the belief system of the Palaeo-Eskimos. The new world view of the Early Dorset people may have perceived a relationship between the methods used by craftsmen and the larger, more mysterious, and more dangerous elements of the universe. The whirling of a drill, for example,

> The permanently frozen floors of Dorset houses provide good conditions for the preservation of organic artifacts. An antler wand carved with images of faces emerges from one such house.

∨ The tiny stone tools of Dorset craftsmen were hafted in handles carved from driftwood and ivory and bound in place with glue and sinew. .

may have been likened to the eddying of snow in a ground-drift driven by winter winds. If drilling were suspected of calling up the wind, the most dangerous element of the weather and a major enemy of Arctic peoples, it may have been deemed safer to abandon the technique, even to ban it from the repertoire of craftsmen. Although this example is fabricated, the disappearance of drilling is more likely to be related to such ideational reasons than to purely functional causes. The phenomenon provides further evidence that the technology and culture of the Dorset people was firmly grounded in a view of the world very different from that of the traditional Inuit or of any inhabitants of the modern world.

A more puzzling disappearance from Dorset technology, and one that must have had much greater significance for the Dorset people, was the bow and arrow. This weapon had much to do with the ability of early Palaeo-Eskimos to occupy Arctic North America. Tiny chipped-stone arrowheads are common finds in the archaeological remains of early Palaeo-Eskimo camps, but the only weapon points found in Dorset sites are so much larger and heavier that they must have been used to tip lances, which were thrown or thrust with the hand. Dorset hunters continued to pursue caribou and muskoxen, the chief quarry of earlier bow hunters, but apparently used lances with large bone heads inset with stone tips and sideblades. The appearance of such lance heads in archaeological collections marks the early phases of Dorset culture throughout the Arctic. Their use must have encouraged the building of drive lanes and drift fences of boulder cairns, which channel caribou toward places where they could be ambushed by hunters. As we noted at the beginning of this chapter, these features of the Arctic landscape are remembered in Inuit tradition as having been built by the Dorset culture Tunit.

As with the drill, the relinquishing of the bow cannot be convincingly explained on grounds of efficiency. We are reminded of the Polar Inuit, a small and isolated band who occupied far northwestern Greenland during the nineteenth century. Over the previous generations, this group had abandoned the use of the bow and arrow, the fish spear, the kayak, and other important elements of traditional Inuit technology. They told early Inuit and European explorers of the area that the use of these artifacts had been lost when an epidemic swept through their small population, killing all of the adult hunters and craftsmen who knew how to construct things such as kayaks and bows. We argued earlier that the early development of Dorset culture occurred during a period of environmental deterioration, when tragedies of starvation must have been relatively common. The bow and arrow may have been abandoned in an atmosphere of crisis surrounding such tragedies, not because all of the bow makers were dead but perhaps because bow hunting was no longer as dependable as other forms of hunting and came to be seen as leading to starvation (Plate 4).

Again we are led to suspect that Dorset people and their way of life cannot be understood from the assumption that they were simple and efficient hunters of animals and creators of artifacts. Their ideas, their concepts of the world, and their belief in how nature functioned force themselves on our attention.

Where Were the Dogsleds and the Kayaks?

The Inuit explorers who contacted the Polar Inuit during the mid-nineteenth century were deeply surprised to encounter a people who lacked kayaks, bows, and other artifacts considered essential to Inuit life. In a similar manner, the first Inuit to encounter the Dorset people of Arctic Canada must have been appalled at the tools and weapons with which these people survived. Again, archaeological evidence supports Inuit traditions regarding the relatively low level of Dorset technology. Again, we puzzle over the reasons why this should have been so.

There is no archaeological evidence, for example, to indicate that the Dorset people used dogsleds. We can be sure that at least some Dorset groups must have had dogs. The pact between humans and dogs was made during the last Ice Age, and the two species have been inseparable ever since. If recently discovered evidence from northern Siberia is correct, dogs may have been pulling sleds for the Arctic peoples of Asia for the past 7,000 years. The first Palaeo-Eskimos to move from Siberia to Arctic North America must have brought dogs with them, and the descendants of these animals would have continued to earn their keep as hunting companions, camp guards, and scavengers. A very few bones of large canines have been recovered from Dorset settlements, and some of these appear to come from wolf-like dogs rather than wolves. But there is none of the complex harness tackle used by Inuit dog handlers and no other evidence that dogs were used to pull sleds. In fact, an amusing Inuit tale of the Tunit relates that these people dressed in bearskins, a material that slides almost frictionless over sea ice; when a man wished to travel, he hooked his dog to the hood of his parka and was pulled along sledless across the ice!

In fact, Dorset people may have occasionally hitched their dogs to the small sleds for which we have archaeological evidence, using a simple leather line without the ivory toggles and swivels favoured by the Inuit. But the scarcity of finds relating to dogs suggests that most Dorset camps possessed few of the animals and that they were not an essential element of transportation. Perhaps the Dorset economy was simply not sufficiently prosperous or secure to support a large dog population. Dogs are the first members of an Arctic camp to suffer during a period of food shortage, and frequent or periodic episodes of starvation may have kept the dog population low.

The scarcity of archaeological evidence for Dorset boats is a more puzzling problem. As in the case of dogs, boat technology extends far back into time, and it was almost certainly available to the first Palaeo-Eskimo migrants to the New World. In fact, archaeological excavations at the Qeqertassusuk site in Greenland dating to early Palaeo-Eskimo times have produced a few broken wooden objects that are almost certainly the ribs from kayak-like boats. Dorset hunters must have known how useful a kayak would be in pursuing sea mammals yet they never developed specialized gear such as that used by the Inuit to hunt from kayaks.

Inuit kayak hunting was associated with a system of float harpoon equipment, in which the harpoon head was attached by line to an inflated sealskin. When an animal was struck, one or more floats and perhaps a drag were thrown overboard; the float served to prevent the animal from diving, to tire it until it could be lanced by the hunter, and to allow it to be retrieved if it sank. Equipment such as this made sea hunting a much more effective and less dangerous enterprise than if the harpoon line was held directly by the hunter. The archaeological remains of Dorset sites produce none of the ivory swivels, toggles, and plugs associated with such harpoon gear. We are left to assume that Dorset hunters must have harpooned animals as large as walrus with a harpoon head attached to a simple line held by the hunter, or perhaps toggled around a sharpened harpoon butt driven into the ice.

Without the complex assemblage of harpoon float gear, Dorset hunters may have considered kayak hunting simply too dangerous and unproductive to be worthwhile. Many such groups may have totally lost the intricate skills associated with constructing skin-covered boats, and kayak building may have survived only tenuously throughout the Dorset world. It is quite possible that the skills died out completely at some periods and were re-introduced through occasional contacts with the kayak-using peoples of the western Arctic.

Where Are Their Dead?

In most parts of the world, the way in which people disposed of their dead provides archaeologists with a great deal of information about how past societies viewed their world and the place of humans in it. A puzzling aspect of Palaeo-Eskimo archaeology is the scarcity of burials associated with this ancient population. Only in Newfoundland, at the sub-Arctic southern limit of Dorset occupation, have human remains been found that are certainly those of Palaeo-Eskimos. Here, local people investigating crevices in limestone cliffs along the western coast of the island have discovered several partial skeletons. The bones are those of Inuit-like people, very similar in physical form to the contemporary peoples of Arctic North America and northeastern Siberia. With them were found Dorset culture artifacts that must have been left either as personal possessions or as gifts to accompany the departed spirit. No such cave burials have been found in any of the Arctic regions occupied by Dorset people. A very small number of boulder structures, which closely resemble the tombs of prehistoric Inuit, have been found to contain both human bones and Dorset culture artifacts. In most cases, a few bones – often mandibles – are the only elements of the skeleton that are found, hinting at the possibility that the Palaeo-Eskimos exposed their dead on the surface and occasionally collected individual bones for more special treatment. We simply don't know what rituals and practices surrounded an act that, in all societies, is fraught with anguish and trepidation.

Dorset Accomplishments

The picture that emerges from archaeological excavation of Dorset settlements depicts a people lacking much of the technology that later Inuit occupants of the Arctic considered essential. Yet without the bow and arrow they were successful hunters of caribou and muskoxen. Lacking kayaks and sophisticated float harpoons, they nevertheless distinguished themselves as superb hunters of seals and walrus. Without extensive use of dogsleds or boats, they maintained a network of trade and an exchange of ideas that spanned most of Arctic Canada and that at times encircled the coasts of Greenland and Newfoundland.

The evidence for long-distance communication comes not only from the extensive dissemination of materials such as jade, native copper, or meteoritic iron but also from the widespread and almost simultaneous changes in artifact styles throughout the Dorset world (Plate 5). For a people so apparently lacking in transportation technology and so closely tied to local resource opportunities, such evidence of continuous communication over a vast area is astonishing. Also surprising is the degree to which Dorset craftsmen throughout the Arctic appear to have followed the dictates of changing fashion, creating tools and weapons that show little stamp of local tradition but that are often indistinguishable from those made thousands of kilometres away.

This exceptional uniformity of style may indicate further the importance that a shared system of beliefs and magico-religious ideas held in Dorset life. Given the evidence that non-functional concepts may have been important in shaping Dorset technology and that mystical qualities may have been ascribed to exotic materials used in that technology, we should perhaps expect the uniformity of Dorset artifacts to reflect a uniformity of beliefs. The importance of magico-religious beliefs and their association with Dorset technology is apparent in the most striking accomplishment of the Dorset people: the creation of a body of art that is unique, unexpected, and remarkable.

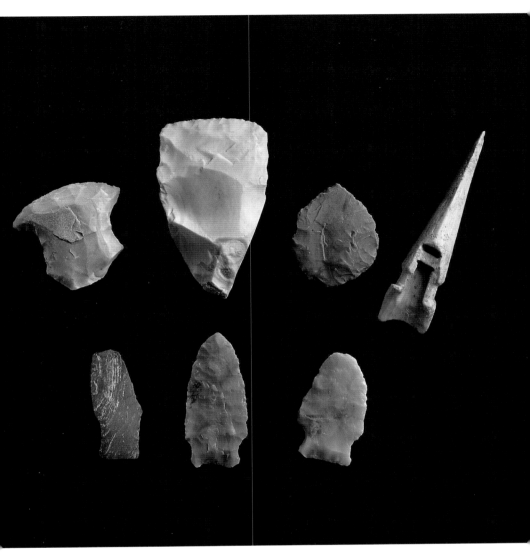

PLATE 1
New styles of artifacts spread across the
Palaeo-Eskimo world during the centuries
between 1000 and 500 BC.

PLATE 2
This wooden figurine representing a man
provides our best information on the clothing of the Dorset people. The figure is
dressed in a double parka with high, three-
sided collar, trousers, and tall boots resembling Inuit kamiks.

PLATE 3
In keeping with Palaeo-Eskimo aesthetic
traditions, Dorset craftsmen carefully
selected the materials they used for tools.
These artifacts (from left, top row: a carving
tool, a harpoon point, a knife blade, three
microblades, and a microblade core) are
chipped from clear quartz crystal. The crystals of rose quartz (bottom row) were also
recovered from a Dorset settlement.

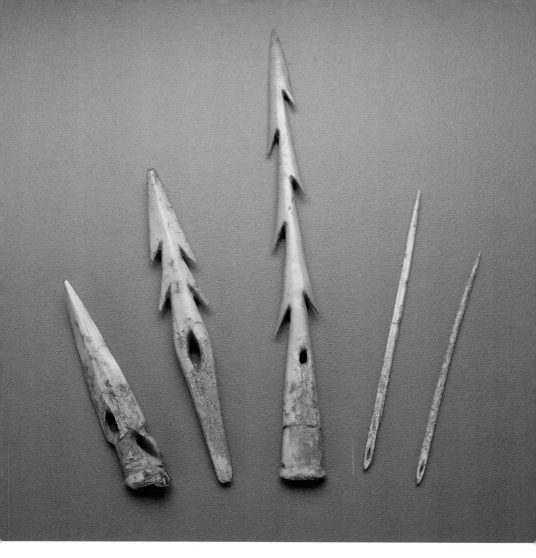

PLATE 4
The Dorset people appear to have abandoned use of the bow, not only as a weapon but also as the propulsive mechanism for drilling holes. In the production of everything from needles to fish spears and harpoons, Dorset craftsmen painstakingly gouged elongated holes rather than drilling circular holes in the manner of their ancestors.

PLATE 5
The Dorset people of Newfoundland were
the most isolated and distant from their
original Arctic homelands. Even here, they
maintained their traditions of fine craftsmanship in chipping these very distinctive
harpoon points from coloured flints. All are
less than five centimetres long.

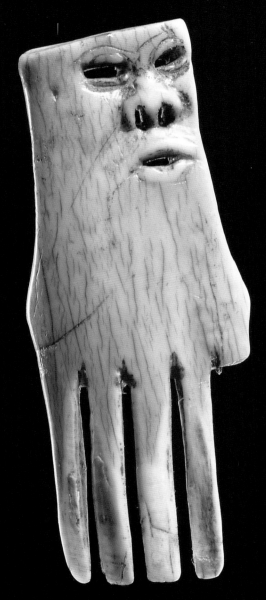

PLATE 6
This fragment of an ivory comb, carved
with the image of a human face, was one of
the earlier pieces of Dorset art to find its
way to a museum.

PLATE 7
The hole in the chest of this small carved
human figure contains a sliver of wood; the
figure may have been ritually killed.

PLATE 8
This ivory maskette, depicting a serene face marked with a complex design that probably represents tattooing, is over 3,500 years old and is the oldest known Palaeo-Eskimo portrait of a human.

PLATE 9
The 'Tyara maskette,' carved approximately
2,000 years ago, hints at an animal-like
quality in the depiction of a human face.

PLATE 10
This ivory 'wolf woman' figure is from
northern Baffin Island.

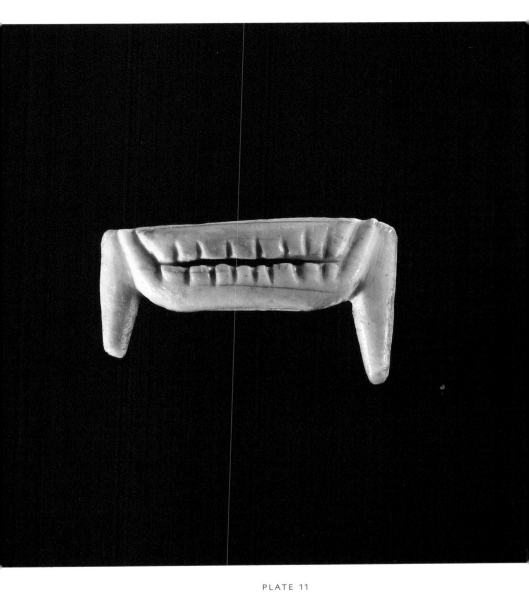

PLATE 11

This set of ivory animal teeth fits the human
mouth and shows tooth marks from ancient
use. A shaman may have used the device to
indicate possession by the spirit of a bear.

PLATE 13
This small carving appears to represent an infant bird, perhaps an owl looking over its back. It was probably worn on a thong threaded through the hole in its tail, its face peering upward at the wearer.

PLATE 14
An ivory carving representing a falcon with
the head of a bear may form an amulet that
combined the powers of these predators.

PLATE 15
This ivory tube is carved in the form of a pair of
walrus, their tusks meeting across the top, and
perforated with holes representing human
faces. This combination of images is found in
settlements from a wide span of Dorset time
and area of occupation.

PLATE 16
This tiny basket, just eight centimetres high, is
the only specimen of its kind recovered from a
Dorset settlement. It was preserved in the per-
manently frozen wall of an early Inuit house at
Brooman Point.

CHAPTER 9

Lost Visions

Archaeologists see themselves as unbiased observers of the past. Like foreign journalists or travel writers, they present the public with an objective and unprejudiced view of distant and alien peoples. Yet inevitably, archaeology's view of the past is heavily prejudiced by the nature of its evidence and of preservation. Past civilizations that built massive structures in stone are much more visible to later generations than are civilizations that built in mud brick or wood. Past cultures that left a legacy of carved stone or painted pottery are appreciated more highly than those that expressed their artistic talents in woven textiles or oral poetry. The massive and sophisticated wood carvings of the Northwest Coast Indians are reduced to powder by one or two centuries of the rainforest environment. If this art had faded before the age of photography and museums, there would be little left in the ground for archaeology to interpret as evidence of a long-cultivated artistic tradition.

The inevitable bias of archaeological interpretation has led us to divide past societies into two groups: the 'great civilizations,' which built henges and pyramids, stone temples and gothic cathedrals; and the others, the 'primitives' and 'precivilized' peoples, whom we assume to have contributed little to the story of human culture. The circumstance of Arctic preservation, however, provides an insight into one of these ancient 'others' and hints at the spiritual thought and artistic ability that must have characterized most such societies.

Like most northern cultures, the Dorset people must have sung songs and created poems, worn elegantly decorated clothing, and tattooed their bodies in intricate patterns. Archaeology provides little evidence of these arts, certainly not enough to distinguish the Dorsets from any other ancient nation. If they had limited their art to such forms, archaeologists would merely consider the Dorsets to have been a rather peculiar people, with unusual attitudes to their technology and to survival in an Arctic environment. But Dorset culture included an element that makes them much more interesting to archaeology: a tradition of carving small figures in hard organic materials that are preserved in the permanently frozen remains of their villages. The preservation of this art not only reveals another side of Dorset culture but also helps to explain many of the otherwise baffling elements of Dorset technology and way of life.

A few tiny ivory carvings were among the artifacts that anthropologist Diamond Jenness received from Arctic Canada in 1924, and on the basis of which he defined the existence of the Dorset culture. These specimens led Jenness to note that 'artistic skill is an ancient heritage of the Eskimos, as old, perhaps, as the people themselves.' Yet Dorset artistic accomplishment attracted little attention for the next forty years. When archaeologists examined the carvings that were a part of most Dorset collections, their interest was primarily in the historical relationships that these objects suggested. Jenness, for example, proposed a possible Dorset ancestry for engraved bone pendants carved by the Beothuk Indians of Newfoundland. Henry Collins, the leading Arctic archaeologist of the interwar period, suggested an affinity between Dorset art and that of the Old Bering Sea culture of Alaska. Graham Rowley, whose 1930s excavations at the Late Dorset site of Abverdjar, near Igloolik, produced the first large sample of Dorset carvings, rejected both of these opinions but offered no alternative interpretation.

By the 1960s, however, the rapidly increasing pace of archaeological work had accumulated approximately 300 Dorset carvings (Plate 6), and this body of art began to capture the attention of scholars. Two finds may have been especially significant in stimulating this interest. In 1961, the ethnologist Bernard Saladin d'Anglure was shown several petroglyph sites on small islands lying off the Arctic coast of Québec. Large clusters of human-like faces, carved into rock outcrops, stared down from cliffs. The faces were large versions of those known from tiny Dorset carvings, and their appearance at localities that must have been places of magical power suggested an important ritual element in Dorset art. The following

An image of a human-like face carved on a
stake of driftwood emerges from the
frozen remains of a Dorset house.

year, the missionary Fr. Guy Mary-Rousselière began to assemble an astonishing collection of wooden artifacts from the eroding coast of Bylot Island: life-sized human masks carved from driftwood, small drum frames, articulated carvings of humans, and animal figures that had been ritually killed with a splinter of wood in the chest or throat (compare with Plate 7). With these surprising finds, archaeologists began to interest themselves in the function of Dorset art and its meaning for our interpretations of the culture.

The change in emphasis did not come easily. In 1960, Danish archaeologist Jorgen Meldgaard's book, *Eskimo Sculpture,* devoted several pages to a description of Dorset art. As for the meaning or function of the art, however, Meldgaard merely noted that some objects may have been carved for entertainment or amusement, while others had 'a definite function in which magic [was] involved.' Writing at approximately the same time about the art objects found at the Early Dorset Tyara site, William E. Taylor Jr. noted that the carvings 'lead into another ill-lit lane of speculation for primitive art is rarely solely *l'art pour l'art.* Were these carvings personal amulets, objects employed for hunting magic, or perhaps part of a shaman's kit? The data offer no new answers to these old questions.' Although the questions may have been old, archaeologists were apparently unwilling to go beyond vague speculation about the answers.

The Silent Echoes: George Swinton and Dorset Art

This reticence was broken in the mid-1960s by George Swinton, the most audacious of the scholars attracted to the Dorset artistic phenomenon. An art historian as well as an avid collector and student of contemporary Inuit art, Swinton approached Dorset carvings as an ancient example of a long-standing Eskimo artistic tradition. In an article entitled 'The Silent Echoes: Prehistoric Canadian Eskimo Art,' published in 1967 as a dialogue with the archaeologist William E. Taylor Jr., Swinton took to task those scholars who simply compared the form and style of Dorset carvings with those made by other societies. He insisted that the 'content' of the art told more about the artistic tradition than did the shape and style of individual carvings.

By 'content,' Swinton seems to have meant the significance that the subject of a piece of art evoked for artist and audience. For example, he considered that a Dorset artist's choice to portray a bear rather than a human, and a flying rather than a walking bear, was more meaningful

This small wooden drum frame is one of two recovered from a Dorset site in the High Arctic, and is associated with other shamanistic equipment.

than the style in which the carving was accomplished. The content of a piece of art, he argued, indicates much more than the manner in which an artist is taught to carve a portrait of an animal. It reflects the entire social context of thought and action in which the work is embedded.

This level of interpretation led Swinton to the conclusion that Dorset carvings were the tangible remnants of a religious tradition. The production of carvings was an integral part of the religious practice of Dorset 'shaman-artists,' and the carvings themselves an essential component of religious ritual and experience:

> We should also like to suggest that the highly developed and exquis-
> itely shaped objects are not the work of occasional carvers, far less
> mere whittlers, but the carefully planned and considered work of
> specialists (either the shamans or their helpers), who knew the tra-
> ditions of form as well as of content, and who applied them in a
> carefully handed down traditional manner. It is by no means unrea-
> sonable to conceive of a Dorset artist-shaman (or a shaman-artist) as
> the main producer of such art.

The concept of the shaman-artist seems to have been derived from the work of Andreas Lommel, who had recently published a book entitled *Shamanism: The Beginning of Art*. Lommel's interest in the religions of hunting peoples lay in their potential for explaining the ancient art painted on the walls of European caves during the last Ice Age. By postulating that religion and art were bound together and by assuming that the religious tradition of twentieth-century hunting peoples was retained from the Palaeolithic period, one could use a study of twentieth-century shamanic art to interpret the art of the European Palaeolithic. To Lommel, 'The shaman is not merely a medicine man, a doctor or a man with priestly functions, he is above all an artistically productive man, in the truest sense of the word creative – in fact, he is probably the first artistically active man known to us.'

We must seriously dispute one of the assumptions – in addition to the notion that all early shamans and artists were male – on which this interpretation is based, namely that religious traditions have remained unchanged among hunting peoples over the past 20,000 years and more. For this entire period, the humans who lived in hunting societies have been as intelligent, curious, and innovative as people in other types of community. Modern urbanites are as close to the occupants of Palaeolithic caves as are the Inuit, the aboriginal peoples of Australia, and other groups whose traditional religions Lommel cites as related to ancient European cave art. For the same reason, although the objection is not nearly as strong, we should question the interpretation of Dorset art in terms of traditional Inuit religion from the past century; the cultural link between Palaeo-Eskimo and Inuit cultures is very tenuous, and any culture can change a great deal in a thousand years or more.

On the other hand, Lommel and other mid-twentieth-century scholars of religion assembled considerable evidence of the traditional religious practices of hunting peoples and were able to demonstrate a basic core of similarities among many of these groups. This core of religious thought – a general view of how the world is constructed, how its forces act and interact, how humans may influence the actions of these forces – came to be termed shamanism and to be thought of as a major world religion. Like all religions, shamanic rituals and practices made use of artifacts created specifically for religious purposes, and as in other major religions many of these artifacts could be termed art objects. George Swinton took this evidence and applied it to the artistic productions of the Dorset people to provide an overall context and explanation for a remarkable collection of archaeological objects. The elegance of Swinton's writing and his ability to instill students and colleagues with his vibrant enthusiasm have created an almost uniform acceptance of his views on Dorset art.

A general interpretation of Dorset carving as an art form that reflects a shamanic view of the world seems reasonably convincing. The religious beliefs held by Dorset people must have fallen somewhere within the range of shamanic beliefs traditionally held by the various hunting societies of Eurasia and North America. It is not as certain, however, that the vast majority of Dorset carvings were created by 'shaman-artists' for a specifically religious use. In fact, the association of Dorset religion and art may not have been as intimate as Swinton suggests. The excellent quality of artistic production does not prove that a relatively small number of skilled carvers were at work but may instead be the result of an unusually high level of carving skill and training among the general Palaeo-Eskimo population. Some Dorset carvings may have been created for purposes as simple as personal adornment – the jewellery of an Arctic people – or for the amusement of children, or to demonstrate the skill of the carver in portraying something seen in the natural world or in a dream. Despite the attractiveness of the idea that Dorset carvings were created by 'shaman-artists,' we should try to keep our minds open to other possibilities as we examine these tiny but splendid objects from the distant past.

The Dorset World

To most of the readers of this book, the earth is a huge round ball spinning slowly through endless icy space, circling a sun that provides the fuel for daylight, wind, rain, and for all living things. We ride the earth through a slowly moving present, a moment that has already advanced through a vast number of years and that will continue forward into an undetermined future. Human life is the result of a long sequence of biological and historical events, through the more ancient of which we are related to all other living things. Trees, insects, animals, and humans share a quality called 'life,' and are distinguished from one another by possession of varying amounts of those qualities we conceptualize as 'strength,' 'mobility,' and 'intelligence.' Living creatures develop from inanimate material and have a defined lifetime, after which they die and gradually disappear once more. Our interactions with the world occur through processes such as physical force, metabolism, and social organization, and we can define and understand these through scientific research. Although some suspect that certain more poorly understood processes – astrological influences, the results of prayer, or extraterrestrial interference – are at work in the world, most see the earth as a more prosaic place.

The Dorset people must have had a very different perception of their world. We can guess at some of its major elements by combining what we know of the world views of other northern peoples and postulating that the Dorset world was similar. Rather than a spinning ball, for example, it was most probably a series of stacked horizontal planes. Humans, caribou, and muskoxen lived on the mid-world, the one about which people understood the most. Above and below were other worlds, inhabited by different classes of creature and where different processes and time scales held sway. For some northern peoples there were only three world planes: an upper world in the sky; the mid-world, where daily activities took place; and an underworld. Other groups lived in universes with up to ten worlds stacked upon one another, linked by a great central tree or by a more vaguely defined series of connections and influences.

We may guess that the Dorset universe had at least four levels: a sky-world inhabited by the sun and moon, stars and planets, the wind and clouds, and doubtless by a host of spirits and forces associated with these elements; the mid-world of earth and ice, on which humans and other animals spent their waking hours; an under-sea and under-ice world of sea mammals, fish, and more poorly known creatures, some of which must have had powers beyond the understanding of the inhabitants of the mid-world; and finally an underworld, below the land and under-sea worlds, evidenced by caves and crevices, the burrows of animals, and phenomena as strange and powerful as the fossil bones of unfamiliar animals and the sulphurous vents of the Smoking Hills. Other and more esoteric levels may have existed as well but were probably more poorly defined and understood.

These diverse worlds must have been inhabited by a great range of creatures, which a twentieth-century mind would divide into several categories: humans; animals and plants; ghosts and other spectral creatures; and spiritual or cosmic forces. A Dorset person would doubtless have thought in terms of different categories, perhaps considering any living creature to combine the qualities of human and animal, spiritual and physical, in much the same way that traditional Christian thought portrays a human being as a combination of a corporeal body and a spiritual soul. Unlike Christian belief, however, shamanic belief does not exclude animals from the world of the spirit. Animals have souls, can become ghosts, and can manifest themselves as spiritual beings. Shamanic thought postulates a distant past when there was no difference between humans and animals, when they could talk to one another and even transform themselves from animal to human form at will. These transformations and communications are thought to occur in the present under special circumstances, such as in a dream or when a human soul journeys to one of the other planes of existence, where the animals live as humans do in the mid-world.

If Dorset thought was similar to that of other shamanic peoples, they must have believed that a human's spiritual powers could be augmented by incorporating the strength and energy of 'helping spirits.' Such spirits could be encountered in dreams, through a deliberately induced trance, or occasionally while hunting or travelling alone on the tundra. Most helping spirits took the shape of animals, and each had specific powers related to the abilities of their animal form: strength, swiftness, subtle cleverness, or the ability to see far beyond the horizon. Through his or her personal helpers, a person could increase ability and luck at hunting, survive dangerous situations, or influence other members of the community.

Although all humans could use such assistants, some individuals acquired much greater abilities at attracting and holding powerful spirit helpers. These men and women were the recognized shamans of the community. Some had been selected at an early age and trained or apprenticed by an elder shaman. Others had been selected by the spirits, usually through recovery from a dangerous and debilitating illness, or perhaps because of a physical or mental abnormality. Still others selected themselves, on the basis of forceful personality and the development of spiritual abilities. Shamans could travel to the other planes of the world in order to contact and influence the world of spirits. They could see events that occurred far beyond the physical horizon, that took place among the animals and spirit people of the sky-world and underworld, or that had not yet happened. With the aid of their spirit helpers they could calm a storm, cure an inexplicable illness, or attract a herd of animals into the range of the community's hunters. The shaman was the doctor, priest, and seer of the small communities of hunters scattered across the Arctic world.

The carvings of the Dorset culture speak eloquently of a shamanic world. The portraits of humans, animals, creatures that appear to be both human and animal, and others that seem to be neither may be thought of as fossilized ideas. These miniature documents have permanently preserved the vision through which Dorset artists perceived their world and the beings that inhabited it. By studying them, we may hope to work out the 'grammar' that Dorset artists used in representing their world.

A Grammar of Animals

In a linguistic sense, grammar refers to the mental system of rules and categories that allows humans to form and interpret the words and sentences of their language. Just as a society shares a set of language rules, they also share a set of meanings that they associate with the various elements of their art. If we treat an artistic tradition as analogous to a language, we may be able to reconstruct some of the meanings behind the various depictions and combinations of depictions that are central to the tradition being studied.

Dorset art is essentially an art that represents individual humans and other animals. All other elements of the environment, many of which have attracted other artistic traditions – landscapes, flowers, scenes of human action, designs based on abstract curvilinear elements – were ignored by Dorset artists, at least insofar as we can tell from what remains. But the choice to portray only individual creatures did not prove to be a limitation; rather, it seems to have opened the way for an exploration of the range of ways in which an animal can be depicted. At one end of this range lie naturalistic miniatures: tiny seals or walrus or bears, which, if they could be expanded perhaps fifty or a hundred times, would be almost perfect replicas of the particular animals portrayed. Then there is a variety of stylized representations, in which creatures are portrayed in ways never seen in the natural world but in such a standardized manner that the artist and audience share the knowledge of what it represents. Farther away from naturalism is a range of abstract portrayals in which a few essential characteristics of an animal are taken to portray the whole – for example, a stylized bear head and sets of claw-marks change a small utensil into an abstract bear. Parts of animals – a caribou hoof, a bear skull, a human foot – represent either the entire animal or a characteristic of the animal that interests the artist. Finally, standardized combinations of animals or animal abstractions obviously had a meaning for the artist and audience, an essential part of the grammar of art shared by Dorset society. As a first step in unravelling this grammar, we can look at the range of depictions of individual species.

Humans and Human-like Beings

The earliest known portrait of a Palaeo-Eskimo is in the form of a small ivory plaque, found on a site that dates to about 3,500 years ago. Only a few centimetres high, this object portrays a serene human face with closed eyes. The forehead, cheeks, and chin are crossed by a series of elegantly curved lines that probably represent tattooing, and the face emanates tranquillity and grace (Plate 8). This is the only known portrait of an early Palaeo-Eskimo individual, who lived long before the development of the Dorset culture. Approximately 1,000 years later, however, very similar faces began to be carved as tiny maskettes by Early Dorset artists.

The most famous of these tiny images was excavated from the Tyara site, an Early Dorset village on the south coast of Hudson Strait. Carved as a miniature mask less than four centimetres high, this portrait has oval eyes and mouth that perforate the thin mask, and a well-modelled straight nose (Plate 9). The face has a tapered oval shape with a narrow chin, while the upper edge of the forehead is concave and rises to a point at either edge. This suggestion of 'ears' projecting from the outer corners of the forehead, combined with the narrowly tapered lower face, gives a vaguely animal-like quality to an image that is essentially and serenely human. The Tyara maskette seems to be a prototype for the tiny masks that are occasionally found in Dorset villages occupied over the following 1,500 years. Over this long period, however, the tranquillity of the Tyara face is usually submerged beneath more animated and harshly delineated features.

The suggestion of animal characteristics in a human face is more apparent in other representations of humans, especially in several small wooden figures, mostly from northern Baffin Island, in which the concave forehead is deepened to a sharp, V-shaped notch flanked by a pair of long, pointed ear-like or horn-like projections, resembling the traditional Christian image of Satan. One small ivory carving from the same region portrays a standing female figure with such well-defined ears and features that she is inevitably recognized as a 'wolf woman' (Plate 10). In another recently discovered carving, an elegantly formed polar bear portrayed in a flying posture has trailing rear legs that are distinctly unbear-like and appear to be human.

Other human figures lack the apparent link with animals but seem to have other ritual associations. Most of these small figurines are carved from driftwood, with crudely fashioned facial features and torsos. Some have no limbs, whereas others have articulated and moveable arms and legs. Among the figures from northern Baffin Island are found a heavily pregnant woman and a fiercely priapic male, suggesting that fertility magic may have been involved in their carving or use. Other figures, scattered throughout the area of Dorset settlement, are distinguished by a slot in the upper chest, sometimes containing a sliver of wood (Plate 7). It is very tempting to view these small and rather chilling objects as the elements of magical acts designed to harm other humans.

Other uses of the human image are suggested by the life-size human masks known from a few Dorset sites. These are carved from driftwood, painted red or black and enlivened with incised tattoo lines and fur eyebrows and moustache attached with pegs. They were most likely worn during ceremonial or ritual activities, probably by shamans engaged in contacting their spirit helpers in order to cure a patient, calm a storm, or predict the location of animals. The mask may have transformed the shaman into a spirit or at least symbolized such a transformation, and the face may not signify a human but a human-like spirit. Carved sets of ivory animal teeth with long, projecting canines like those of a bear or wolf probably represent other transformations; these have been designed to be placed in the front of the mouth, where they can be gripped by the teeth and give a quite uncannily effective impression of a human face becoming that of an animal (Plate 11).

The most bizarre representations of humans are found in clusters of faces carved into the surface of chunks of caribou antler. These oddly shaped wands or batons have been recovered from several Late Dorset villages. Some have only a few faces distributed over their surface; others are completely covered, with up to sixty faces jostling for position. Some of the faces seem to exemplify rather ordinary humans but others do not. There are impossibly long faces with incredibly narrow and elegant noses, broad and squat faces with grimacing mouths and wild hair; faces with the lips rounded and projected as if blowing their breath at the observer; faces with animal muzzles; and others with wide open screaming mouths and protruding tongues. We can only guess at the interpretation of these crowds of tiny faces. They may be cartoon-like representations of the people who lived in a local community, or perhaps images of a Dorset pantheon of spirit beings, or the spirit helpers controlled by the individual shamans who owned and used these artifacts. One of the more spectacular examples is heavily worn around a zone that fits well into the hand, and it must have been habitually carried in order to accumulate such damage (Plate 12).

Some of the same faces portrayed on masks and wands are found in the petroglyphs carved into rock cliffs along the coasts of Hudson Strait. The rock carvings, the multifaced antler wands, the wooden masks, the small wounded figures, and the human-animal images all suggest that Dorset artists used human imagery primarily in the service of magical or spiritual power. Taken together, the assemblage of human representations leaves the observer with a distinctly uneasy impression. The calm serenity apparent in the tiny maskettes carved during the early centuries of the Dorset period soon disappears, to be replaced by a variety of images ranging from unsettling to bizarre.

Even the few images that at first glance appear simply naturalistic and even charming have some unusual characteristics. A wooden figure of a man, found in a High Arctic site, seems designed to portray the clothing of the Dorset people: a double parka with straight lower edges, trousers and high boots, or *kamiks*, closely resemble Inuit clothing, except that the parka hood is replaced by a high standing collar; on closer examination the grotesquely pursed and blowing lips seem to portray either a ritual action or the mark of a non-human creature. A similar ivory carving from Greenland shows the same combination of blowing mouth and high, three-sided collar but a naked body. Two small ivory figures from the Igloolik area are usually cited as the most charming of Dorset human representations: both show a man with an infant, one sitting on his shoulders and the other standing on his shoulders while the man tilts his head back and looks up at the child. Perhaps these are simple representations of normal human activities, yet when one looks closely at the broad shoulders and rather malevolent face of the 'child,' one wonders whether the image may not represent a man forced to bear the burden of a heavy and malignant spirit creature. Such an interpretation would be more consistent with the remainder of the Dorset artistic corpus, in which humans are portrayed as actors in a magical world of animals and spirits rather than as people engaged in the everyday acts of living.

Bears and Bear Spirits

Aside from human and human-like faces, the commonest image in Dorset art is the bear, the most powerful predator of the Dorset world. The polar bear must have been perceived by the Palaeo-Eskimos as the animal that most closely resembled themselves. Only bears and humans hunted sea mammals, and bears were the only creatures besides other humans that posed occasional threats to human life. The skeleton of a dead bear – the essential and most spiritually potent portion of the anatomy in shamanic thought – so nearly resembles the human skeleton that a close kinship seems obvious. Observing a bear skeleton on an Arctic beach, one easily conceives of the bear as a human equipped with a heavy white coat and a mighty head specialized for seal killing. As a particularly powerful form of human-like creature, the bear must also have been seen as an exceptionally influential spirit creature, capable of rendering great assistance or great harm to humans who came into contact with it.

Bears are portrayed in a spectacular array of forms. These examples include a 'portrait' head; a remarkably detailed and correct skull; an animal in a floating or flying posture, which may represent a spirit-bear; and a very abstracted animal in the same posture.

Dorset artists portrayed bears in many ways; indeed, the range of art from naturalistic to stylized and various degrees of abstraction is best illustrated in the treatment of bears. At one end are occasional carvings of what appear to be individual bears standing, swimming, or sitting like dogs. These rare portraits, elegantly proportioned and with finely detailed faces, have the charm so conspicuously lacking in the images of humans. There is no hint that these objects had any use other than to delight artists and their audience in the miniature portrayal of an element of the natural world.

More common, however, are figures in a highly stylized fashion that suggests the spiritual power of the bear rather than the animal itself. These animals are depicted with the hind legs stretched backward and the forelegs trailing alongside the body, suggesting that the bear is floating or perhaps flying. A formalized pattern incised on the surface of the body seems to represent an abstract skeleton: vertebrae and ribs are indicated, major joints are designated by plus signs, and an X marks the top of the skull. We may suspect that these carvings represent the powerful spirit helper of a shaman, or perhaps the shaman possessed by a spirit helper and travelling on a quest to another realm of the universe. Flying bear representations have been recovered from Dorset villages across the eastern Arctic, indicating a widely shared cluster of spiritual concepts and artistic conventions. Many of them are stylized to a greater or lesser extent and some are reduced to flat, plaque-like forms retaining only the bear's head, some of its skeletal markings, or the outline of its limbs.

Several Dorset villages from different regions have produced detailed and naturalistic carvings of bear heads, perforated at the neck to be attached to cords or clothing and probably worn as amulets. A variant on this theme is a tiny bear skull only twenty-five millimetres long, the same size as the complete bear heads and finished in every detail except that the long canine teeth have been snapped off. At such a cultural distance, it is impossible to reconstruct the meaning that such objects held for the Palaeo-Eskimos who carved, used, or wore them. Nevertheless, it is clear from the number of bear images produced by Dorset artists and the variety of forms that such images took that the bear was perceived as an extremely powerful and interesting creature. The help and protection of a polar bear must have been highly valued.

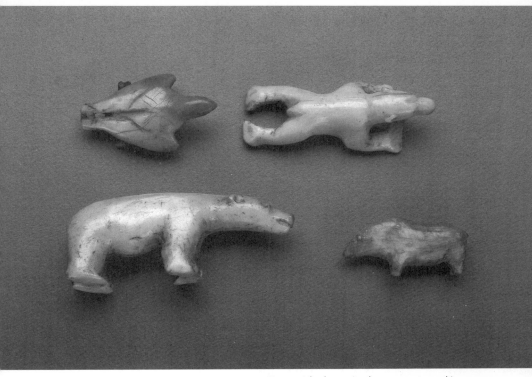

Bears and other animals were portrayed in realistic as well as abstracted forms. This series of small ivory carvings representing bears, a muskox, and a diving falcon with outstretched talons is from a single Late Dorset settlement.

Spirit Raptors

Birds are another favoured subject of Dorset artists. Representations of birds seem to be more varied, and to be relatively free of the widespread artistic conventions applied to humans and bears. Some of the images are among the most attractive and engaging of Dorset carvings: an alert ptarmigan; a young owl with its head turned completely backwards to look over its tail (Plate 13); a swooping falcon with talons extended to grasp its prey; a nesting eider duck with her eggs carved against her belly. Images of geese and swans are well represented, as might be expected for the largest and tastiest of Arctic waterfowl. Most have a tiny suspension hole through the tail, however, indicating that they were worn as decoration or more likely as amulets and suggesting that some other characteristic of these large birds – perhaps their ability for swift and powerful flight – might have been more important to their Dorset owners. Birds of prey, in the form of falcons, are also carved as naturalistic amulets, and in these cases we may suspect an attempt to transfer the hunting ability of the bird to the human who wore its image.

Other raptor images are not as simply representational but partake of stylized conventions similar to those found in representations of bears. All of these birds appear to embody falcons, but it is unclear which of the two prime raptors of the Arctic – the gyrfalcon or the peregrine – is portrayed. The birds are carved with their wings folded but slightly open as they are carried in a diving attack. The heads are well modelled and naturalistic, except in the case of one specimen with a finely carved bear head attached to the falcon body (Plate 14). The underside of the bird seems to be pictured as a skeleton.

Although the skeletal motif suggests similarities between the stylized images of falcons and bears, there is a more striking congruence between the form of the falcons and that of a prominent type of Dorset harpoon head, probably used primarily for hunting walrus. These elegant weapons expand from a pointed tip to a pair of thin and slightly spread wings ending in sharp spurs; the upper surface is smoothly rounded, while the undersurface is hollowed out on either side of a prominent central keel, which contains the hole through which the harpoon line is attached. When placed side by side on their 'backs' with their 'bellies' exposed, the relationship between harpoon head and falcon is obvious. It seems clear that to a Dorset hunter and carver these harpoon heads were metaphorical falcons or skeletal falcon spirits poised to make the kill that was so important to a hunter's welfare. The carvings of falcons or falcon spirits themselves must have had other significance, either as representations of a shaman's swift and far-ranging spirit helper or as containers of the spiritual power required to safely and successfully take animals as large and dangerous as the walrus.

Portraits of the Hunted

Bears and falcons, the most striking predators of the Dorset world, are perhaps the most obvious subjects for a hunting people to represent in their art. The arctic wolf, the other major hunter of the north, is rarely seen in the lands occupied by the Dorset people, being closely associated with the caribou herds of the Arctic mainland regions, which were marginal to Dorset occupation. Others, such as foxes or gulls, are more often seen as scavengers and were probably not thought worthy of frequent portrayal. Only one other tiny predator, the weasel, was impressive enough to be represented occasionally.

Most other animals must have been viewed primarily in their role as prey for human hunters. These works of art include at least one example of almost every creature known to the Dorset people, and many species are seen in a wide variety of portrayals. The images of prey animals seem to be much less limited by stylistic convention than those of bears and falcons.

Seal and walrus are the most commonly portrayed species, but they are depicted in quite different manners. Most seal carvings are naturalistic in form, perfect miniatures that look as if they are either swimming or sleeping on the ice. Heads and flippers are so perfectly sculpted that one can often recognize the species of seal portrayed, while on the smallest carvings the eyes, nostrils, ears, mouth, and even nipples are delineated by tiny lines or dots. In contrast, walrus carvings are not naturalistic but occur in a variety of stylized forms, suggesting that they may have been widely linked with shamanic activities. Walrus are also portrayed in association with other animals, as we shall see in a later section.

Few depictions of whales are known in Dorset art. Beluga whales are represented by only a couple of small carvings, no carvings of narwhals have been found, and we know of only one depiction of a large bowhead whale. Fish are also poorly represented, aside from one rather unexpected type: the sculpin. These small and fantastically shaped creatures seem to have fascinated Dorset artists, and carved images of sculpins have been recovered from several sites. We might imagine that the sculpin featured in Dorset stories as a mysterious inhabitant of the undersea world, perhaps as a messenger to the more powerful denizens of that strange and hidden universe that was so important as a source of food for the Dorset people.

The animals of the land are much more poorly represented in the repertoire than are the sea mammals, among which polar bears are classed. Although Dorset hunters did take caribou and muskoxen, these animals may have been perceived as less mysterious or less dangerous than the creatures of the sea and perhaps not as potent in magical qualities. The muskox is portrayed in only one known carving, a tiny sketch in ivory that unmistakeably reproduces the rounded silhouette of the creature but shows no details. No known carving portrays an entire caribou, but the animal is occasionally represented by a part of its anatomy, usually the hoof and lower leg. Carved in great detail, and sometimes bearing an incised skeletal motif, these objects are usually in the form of amulets perforated for attachment to clothing or to a suspension cord; they may have been designed to provide the wearer with a measure of the fleetness of a caribou.

Combining the Powers of Animals

Some of the more interesting representations of animals are found on small tubes and containers, which were produced in very standardized forms but for functions that we do not understand.

One of these types of utensil is a simple hollow cylinder, either cut from a long bone or carved from an ivory tusk. This type of tube has a skeleton design, suggesting that it is a stylized animal, and one end is cut by a pair of deep, V-shaped notches forming what appears to be the animal's yawning mouth. To further this impression, an animal face is carved on this portion of the tube. But rather than simply depicting the face and jaw of a single creature flanking the open mouth, each side carries the image of a different animal: a wolf on one side and on the other a caribou. One wonders whether this juxtaposition of predator and prey had a significance in the Dorset grammar of animals.

Another type of artifact, just as mysterious in its function, was also widely used throughout the Dorset world. These are small, hollow

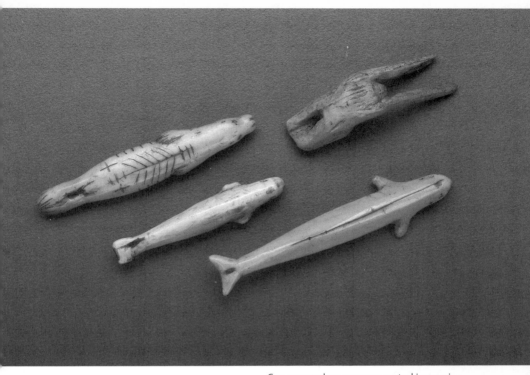

Sea mammals were represented in a variety of forms. These examples include two realistic beluga, a seal with a visible skeleton, and the head of a walrus.

containers carved from ivory, usually from the proximal end of a walrus tusk. They are known to have been used over a period of 2,000 years or more, first appearing during the transitional period that was to lead to the development of Dorset culture. The form changed considerably over time. With a flattened bell shape, they have an oval cross-section expanding from a thin rounded end to a broad opening at the other extremity. In their final form, the narrower edges of the oval are carved as a pair of walrus with their tusks meeting across the top of the object; the broader sides of the flattened bell carry depictions of human faces, formed by sets of perforations, and sometimes a small animal is carved above the face on one of the sides. The combination of paired walrus with two human faces and another small animal must have had a symbolic meaning within the Dorset system of beliefs and symbols, but that meaning eludes us. Similarly elusive is the function of these small artifacts. They may have been used as containers for small items of magical equipment, or perhaps as rattles, instruments widely associated with shamanic practices (Plate 15).

The small sculptures produced by Dorset artists obviously portray a world in which animals were a central focus, in which certain animals were especially valued for their spiritual powers or other magical qualities, and in which animals could occasionally show a human face or humans display some of the attributes of animals. It is clear, however, that we can only guess at most of the 'grammar of animals' through which the artists understood the symbolism and magical forces represented in their sculptures.

Magic Weapons?

Other glimpses of Dorset spiritual belief and practice can be obtained from the few other classes of artifacts that seem to be associated with magical activities or religious ritual. Most numerous of these are tiny harpoon heads, many of them less than one centimetre long and far too small to have functioned as ordinary weapons. Most of these specimens, however, are precise replicas of the large harpoon heads used to kill walrus or seals. We do not know how they were used; perhaps some of them were children's toys; others may have been amulets designed to help in the hunt. A more likely function, however, can be reconstructed from our knowledge of shamanic theories of illness, in which pain and disease can be sent to an individual by an enemy. One of the techniques used by shamanic healers to cure people afflicted in this way involves the removal of the offending weapons from the patient's body, often by sucking them through the skin with a special tube or container similar to those described in the previous section. Perhaps the majority of the tiny harpoon heads found in Dorset villages were such magic weapons, used by a shaman to demonstrate the cause of an illness that had been cured. Of course, there is also the more sinister possibility that some of these miniature weapons may have been used in rituals designed to send illness or death to an enemy, rather than to cure.

Certain other Dorset carvings or utensils that do not have an obvious function may also have had magical purposes. Among such items are flat, double-pointed pieces of wood, carefully shaped and often incised with an animal skeleton design; numerous small, spatula-like objects, often in the form of stylized animals, usually bears; and small, bilobate carvings variously resembling dumbbells, spectacle rims, or human breasts.

Finally, one archaeological site in northern Baffin Island has produced two fragments of drums. Throughout the shamanic world, the tambourine-like drum is the 'shaman's steed,' or the 'door to the world of spirits.' It is the means by which shamans induce the trance state that allows them to travel to distant realms and converse with strange and powerful beings. The Dorset drum rims are tiny, only about twenty centimetres across, and could not have produced the hypnotic booming roar of large Inuit drums. Their diminutive size accords with the emphasis on miniaturization that pervades Palaeo-Eskimo culture, and their relatively high-pitched tone may have been as effective as that of a larger drum in allowing shaman and audience to accomplish a hypnotic state. Combined with wooden masks in the flickering lamplight, fantastically carved wands and containers, tiny weapons, and the elegantly sculpted images of powerful spirits, drumming must have been an effective weapon to a small and isolated community facing a frightening world.

Dorset Art and the Shamanic World

The universe of the Dorset people was very different from ours. It was as dangerous a place as is our own world – a place where accidents, misfortunes, and illness visit people for reasons beyond human understanding – but the means of coping were not what we would consider effective. In the explanations developed above, most of the carvings found in the remains of Dorset villages can be associated with magical or religious means of dealing with a shamanic universe.

Most students of Dorset art eventually reach this type of interpretation, and it provides a relatively satisfying sense that we have penetrated the mysteries of the art and gained insight into the world view it represents. But beyond such feelings of satisfaction, we must recognize that much of Dorset art will always remain mysterious. Part of the problem must lie in our definition of this vast range of sculpted artifacts as art. What does an antler wand covered with dozens of sinister faces have in common with the charming effigy of a plump ptarmigan? Are miniature harpoon heads a part of the same art form as the ivory portraits of seals and swans and standing bears? A Dorset individual probably saw these as completely different classes of technology, perhaps no more closely linked than wristwatches, pocket calculators, and eyeglasses are for us. Some may have been closely identified with healing, like stethoscopes and hypodermics in our society. Some may have been relied on for the type of help in hunting that we obtain from binoculars or electronic fish-finders. Some perhaps were used in much the same way that we would use a compass, to protect their owners from becoming lost on the tundra or off a foggy coast.

Still others may have had no practical purpose in the life of the community but have been the simple products of artists' impulses to reproduce their world, or their dreams, through their own thoughts and actions. The uniformly fine craftsmanship apparent in tools and weapons, which would probably have been made by most individuals in a community, suggests that Dorset society was characterized by a high level of technical competence. Many people in a village must have been capable of turning out competently carved and finely finished figures and of giving scope to the impulses of an artist. Given such a background, it seems unlikely that Dorset art was a single class of activity practised by a few specialized 'shaman-artists.'

Some sculptures were obviously created by individuals who would be identified in any society as artists of talent and vision. Many others were produced by people whose level of technical competence in working small pieces of ivory or wood was far superior to that found in most modern societies. A remarkably small number of carvings were made by individuals who were reasonably competent but who lacked the ability to make an animal look quite real. When we first see the material that we define archaeologically as Dorset art, we are overwhelmed by the sheer existence of such miniature artistry. On closer examination, we begin to detect a wider range of abilities. This is perhaps another argument to suggest that their tiny carvings may have been perceived by the Dorset people as representing several types of artifacts: medical instruments, magical weapons, personal ornaments, perhaps even playthings. Surviving into our own world, they merge into a single phenomenon, an art form that is the most potent and delightful remnant of an ancient way of life.

CHAPTER 10

Encounters and Isolation

For over 3,000 years the many small bands of Palaeo-Eskimos scattered across the tundra of Arctic Canada and Greenland sustained a remarkably uniform culture and way of life. Changes in the styles of harpoon heads, knives, or carvings representing bear spirits occurred at roughly the same time over distances of thousands of kilometres. We can imagine that new clothing styles, songs, and stories were also spread through a vast and tenuous network of accidental encounters between hunters, seasonal meetings arranged with adjacent bands, and occasional journeys undertaken by traders or explorers. The homogeneity of style, in turn, must have fostered a feeling of identity, of solidarity in the face of alien people, among the small and scattered bands of the Palaeo-Eskimos.

The existence of such a coherent culture strongly suggests that all of the Palaeo-Eskimo peoples spoke a single language 4,000 to 5,000 years ago. Distinctive dialects must have emerged in local populations, isolated from one another for most months of every year. Nevertheless, neighbouring groups would have comprehended one another's speech with ease, and travellers to more distant lands could probably have made themselves understood. The movement of soapstone, jade, native copper, and meteoritic iron throughout the Palaeo-Eskimo world is an archaeological indication that ideas and new knowledge were also shared by groups from the Barren Grounds to the Greenland fiords and southward through the forests of Labrador and Newfoundland.

The gradual changes undergone by Palaeo-Eskimo culture, including the development of the Dorset way of life, are interpreted as products of this far-ranging exchange of knowledge and ideas. Given the apparent facility with which ideas spread across the Palaeo-Eskimo population, we might ask whether all such ideas originated among the Palaeo-Eskimos themselves or whether some were acquired through contacts with peoples of other cultural traditions: Alaskan Eskimo populations, the Indian peoples of the northern forests, and in later times the Norse who settled Greenland and made occasional forays along the coasts of northeastern Canada.

Early Alaskans
Palaeo-Eskimos were the first people to achieve a widespread occupation of Alaska's Arctic coasts and tundra plains. Some groups spread east to become the earliest inhabitants of Arctic Canada and Greenland, while others remained to develop an Alaskan cultural tradition that lasted for almost two thousand years. Known to archaeologists as the Denbigh Flint Complex, the tiny stone tools recovered from these early camps are practically indistinguishable from those found in early Palaeo-Eskimo sites in the eastern Arctic. The oldest Denbigh sites may date to as early as 3000 BC; the latest seem to have been occupied at some time between 1500 and 1000 BC. The Alaskan Denbigh Flint Complex is therefore contemporary with, as well as very similar to, the early Palaeo-Eskimo tradition of Arctic Canada and Greenland.

Such parallel developments from a common ancestor were not to continue. In the eastern Arctic, the millennium beginning about 1000 BC saw the period of widespread disruption that transformed the early Palaeo-Eskimo tradition into the Dorset culture. These events have been interpreted as involving a single continuing population, which was subjected to the rigours of a deteriorating environment and accomplished an efficient and very successful adaptation to their new circumstances. Alaskan cultures underwent even more dramatic changes during the same period, but some or all of these changes may have been due to the appearance of new populations with different cultural traditions.

The coastal regions of western and northern Alaska, the homelands of the Denbigh people, were closely bounded by zones with vastly different environmental characteristics, inhabited by peoples of different cultural traditions. The forests of western Alaska approach close to the coastline, and the forests and rivers were the homes of various Indian groups. Across Bering Strait, northeastern Siberia was occupied by peoples whose

Contacts between the Palaeo-Eskimos and
the Algonkian-speaking groups of the eastern sub-Arctic are suggested by a variety of
hints. This nineteenth-century ceremonial
structure built by the Cree on the coast of
Hudson Bay bears an intriguing resemblance to the longhouses constructed by
the Dorset people.

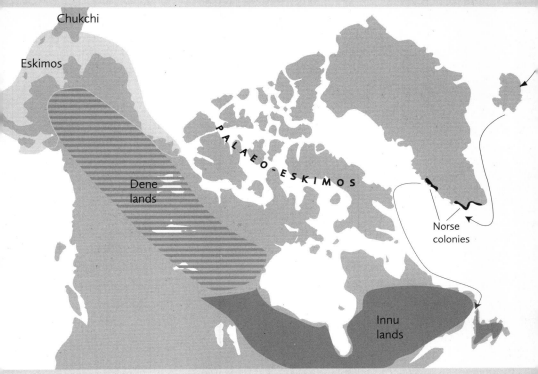

Chukchi

Eskimos

Dene
lands

PALAEO-ESKIMOS

Norse
colonies

Innu
lands

MAP 10.1
Neighbouring peoples during the Late
Dorset period, after AD 1000

technologies and economies were increasingly influenced by the Bronze and Iron Age civilizations of China and Mongolia. Perhaps most important, the coasts of the North Pacific Rim – the coasts from California to northern Japan – were home to a continuous series of ancestral maritime hunting cultures.

After 1500 BC archaeological sites in western and northern Alaska began to exhibit an accelerating process of cultural and technological change. New technologies appeared, seemingly through contacts with several adjacent regions. People who continued to use the chipped-stone tools of the Denbigh Flint Complex also began to make ceramic pots and lamps similar to those of Siberia, as well as tools of ground and polished stone closely resembling those long used by peoples of the Pacific coast. The tundra regions between the forest and the Arctic coast were occupied by groups using such a mixture of technologies that it is difficult to distinguish ancestral Eskimo from ancestral Indian cultures. Instead of the slow and steady progression of cultural change that characterized the Palaeo-Eskimo tradition in the eastern Arctic, Alaskan coasts were occupied by a succession of peoples using tools and weapons quite different from those of the groups they displaced.

The Choris People

One of the more intriguing groups is named Choris, after a small peninsula just north of Bering Strait where a group of very large oval houses were excavated to reveal a previously unknown culture. The sites occupied by Choris people are found throughout northwestern Alaska and date between approximately 1500 and 500 BC. Choris technology shows an interesting combination of chipped-stone tools apparently derived from the Denbigh tradition, Siberian pottery, a few tools of polished stone, and the first evidence for a relatively efficient maritime hunting technology in the regions north of Bering Strait. The great abundance of caribou bones on many Choris sites led Louis Giddings, who first defined the culture, to suggest that the Choris people may also have experimented with herding reindeer on the pattern followed by later Siberian groups. Few archaeologists have taken this suggestion seriously, and most consider that the Choris people were simply efficient hunters of caribou as well as of seals and beluga whales.

The Choris culture remains very much a mystery. Is it a missing link between earlier Palaeo-Eskimo cultures and later groups that were directly ancestral to the Eskimo peoples of Alaska, or is it simply a diverse technology that marks the end of the Palaeo-Eskimo tradition? If we are uncertain of the place of Choris culture in Alaskan history, its possible contribution to the history of eastern Arctic peoples is even more obscure. The Choris period spans the end of the early Palaeo-Eskimo phase in the eastern Arctic and the transitional period that saw the development of Dorset culture. Several elements of Choris technology, such as polished stone burins and ground slate knives, appear as innovations in Early Dorset culture; both Choris and Dorset are marked by the appearance of a more efficient form of marine hunting economy. We have generally thought that despite these similarities the almost 2,000 kilometres between Alaskan Choris sites and the westernmost Dorset site on Victoria Island precluded any possible relationship between the two, but a Choris culture site has recently been found at the northeastern edge of the Mackenzie Delta, about 1,000 kilometres east of the concentration of Choris sites in northwestern Alaska. Some of the artifacts at this site are made from stone that comes from deposits a couple of hundred kilometres farther east. Suddenly, the geographical distance between Choris and Dorset sites has been cut by more than half, and we may begin to suspect that the two have a historical relationship.

No evidence of Dorset occupation has been found in the western Canadian Arctic, a vast stretch of low rolling plains between the Mackenzie and Coppermine rivers. Yet two large sites from this area – one on the Cape Bathurst Peninsula and one on Banks Island, over a hundred kilometres across Amundsen Gulf to the north – indicate that the area was occupied between roughly 500 BC and AD 1. The artifacts made by the people living in this region, known to archaeologists as the Lagoon Complex, show a strange mixture of traits resembling early Palaeo-Eskimo, Dorset, Choris, and Choris-like Alaskan cultures. It seems likely that the Choris occupation of regions as far east as the Mackenzie Delta gave rise to this Alaskan-influenced culture in areas immediately to the east. It is also conceivable that occasional contacts between these people and ancestral Dorset people in the central Arctic may have provided the opportunity for transferring some technological ideas: grinding and polishing stone to produce more even and durable edges than could be achieved by flaking; or perhaps the shallow excavation of house floors to

The ice-free coasts of southern Alaska
have long been occupied by maritime
hunting peoples living from the rich
marine environments of the northern
Pacific. This was probably the original
homeland of the Eskimos, and the central
genius of Eskimo culture was the adaptation of this economy to the ice-covered
waters of the Bering and Chukchi seas.

These small stone tools and fragments of
pottery were recently recovered from a
Choris culture site in the Mackenzie Delta.
They suggest a possible link between the
development of Dorset culture and the
evolving cultural traditions of Alaska.

provide extra protection from cold and wind. Although absolutely no archaeological evidence of boats has been recovered from either Choris or Early Dorset sites, it is tempting to suggest the re-introduction of a kayak-like hunting boat as an explanation for the apparent increase in maritime hunting efficiency in the Dorset culture of the eastern Arctic.

The isolated transfer of a few limited technological ideas, however, seems very different from the spread of new styles throughout the Dorset world. Most elements of Dorset technology developed out of the early Palaeo-Eskimo tradition of the eastern Arctic, and there is no indication in Dorset art of new aesthetic ideals or religious concepts from the peoples to the west. From what we know of the rates at which languages change, by around 2,000 years ago the long isolation of ancestral Dorset people in the eastern Arctic must have given rise to a language that was incomprehensible to any other Palaeo-Eskimo populations. If contacts did occur between Dorset groups and the Choris-like or Choris-derived peoples to the west, they must have occurred across linguistic as well as geographical borders. Relations were thus probably very wary if not overtly hostile, and not conducive to the wholesale adoption of ideas.

Eskimo History

The history of Alaska during the first millennium BC is very blurred and indistinct. The millennium begins with the Arctic coasts and tundra in the hands of peoples of apparent Palaeo-Eskimo ancestry; when it ends, the same areas are firmly held by groups clearly ancestral to the Eskimos of today. The transition between these states is quite unclear.

One interpretation of this period sees Palaeo-Eskimos gradually transformed into Eskimos, through a long process of absorbing technologies and cultural ideas from nearby inhabitants of Asia and the North Pacific coasts. By the end of the millennium, ancestral Eskimos living in the vicinity of Bering Strait had accumulated the basic features that were to distinguish Eskimo culture from that of neighbouring groups: an efficient maritime economy adapted to seasonally frozen Arctic seas, based on the use of skin-covered boats and complex harpoon equipment; and a society centred on large, permanent communities of log and turf winter houses, heated and lit by lamps burning the oil of sea mammals. In addition, these people of the Old Bering Sea culture had evolved an elaborate artistic tradition, focused on the decoration of weapons and tools with complex animal designs. Together, these developments had produced a culture and way of life so far removed from the ancestral Palaeo-Eskimo tradition that the relationship between the two can barely be recognized.

A second interpretation suggests that there is no direct ancestral relationship between the Eskimo cultures of 2,000 years ago and the Palaeo-Eskimo cultures of a millennium earlier. According to this view, the ancestors of the Eskimos were a people of the North Pacific Rim, occupying the southern coast of Alaska and the adjacent Aleutian Islands since shortly after the Ice Age. This explanation has the advantage of placing ancient Eskimos in a region adjacent to the one occupied for the past several millennia by their linguistic and cultural relatives, the Aleuts. The development of an Arctic Eskimo culture would have occurred during the final millennium BC, as some of these peoples moved north along the coasts of the Bering Sea, learning from their Palaeo-Eskimo predecessors in this area and adapting their North Pacific maritime hunting technology to the seasonally ice-covered waters of the Arctic regions.

Neither variant of early Eskimo history is particularly relevant to the story of the Dorset people of the eastern Arctic. After the period of possible contact between Choris and Dorset groups along the coasts of Amundsen Gulf, there is no evidence to suggest any communication between the Dorset Palaeo-Eskimos of the east and the evolving Eskimo tradition of Alaska. The first millennium AD saw an acceleration in the rate of Alaskan cultural development. The Eskimo way of life that had been well established in the Bering Strait area by the beginning of the millennium spread north to the Chukchi Sea coasts of both Alaska and Siberia and south to overwhelm the earlier traditions of Alaska's Pacific coast. Among the notable accomplishments of this period was the development of efficient whaling techniques, which allowed the Eskimos to successfully hunt bowhead whales, the largest creatures of the Arctic seas. In particularly productive hunting locations, such as the points of land extending from the northern coast of Alaska into the migratory paths of the whales, very large communities developed. Another accomplishment was the growth of widespread trade centred on iron, which reached the area from the civilizations of central and eastern Asia.

Together, these developments defined the Thule culture, an Eskimo way of life that by AD 1000 was centred on the northwestern coast of Alaska and that was capable of rapid expansion. This capability was to

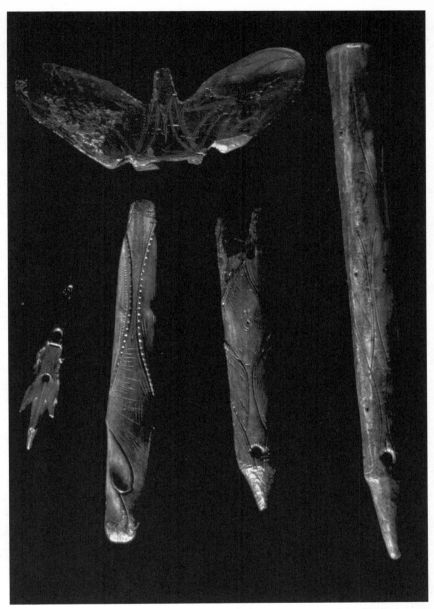

The hunting weapons of the Old Bering Sea culture, excavated from an ancient settlement near Bering Strait, carry complex designs that follow an entirely different artistic tradition from Palaeo-Eskimo art.

Archaeologists examine the eroding face of an ancient Eskimo settlement at Bering Strait, where animal bones and the ruins of houses have accumulated to a depth of several metres. The large number of whale bones in the deposit testify to centuries of stable economic conditions in a rich environment.

become of momentous importance to the Dorset people, whose traditional culture and economy, little changed from that of their ancestors, still sustained their scattered population throughout the coasts and islands of the eastern Arctic.

Northern Indians

At the middle of the twentieth century, northern North America was considered to hold potential answers to many questions of American prehistory. The region was an archaeological vacuum that might hold traces of migrations between the Old and New Worlds or of the spread of technologies such as ceramics or ground and polished stone. Prevalent theories on ethnic origins suggested that the area might provide evidence of Eskimo cultures developing from an interior Indian way of life or of an Eskimo ancestry for early Indian cultures known archaeologically from regions as far south as the Great Lakes. Lacking the time scale that would soon be provided by the radiocarbon dating technique, archaeologists tended to collapse the major events of North American prehistory – such as the developments of agriculture and the ceramic arts or the evolution of Eskimo culture – into the past few centuries or millennia.

This was the intellectual environment into which the first scattered remnants of Dorset culture were introduced. These small and finely made tools were so different from the technology of any known Eskimo culture that archaeologists began to look elsewhere for possible relationships. Similarities were soon noted between the ground slate tools of Dorset culture and those used by the ancient peoples of the Great Lakes region, a vague resemblance that led to much conjecture. Even when radiocarbon dating proved that the Archaic Indian technologies were several millennia older than those of the Palaeo-Eskimos and that the similarities must be purely coincidental, the sense of a possible relationship remained. In the early 1960s, when Jorgen Meldgaard excavated the long sequence of Palaeo-Eskimo occupations at Igloolik, he characterized the Dorset material that he recovered as 'smelling of the forest.' Decades later, with a much greater amount of information and more precise dating of the Indian cultures of the northern forests, it may be worth reassessing these impressions of earlier archaeologists.

During the past few centuries, the zone of contact between Indian and Inuit cultures was divided into two major regions: from Bering Strait to the west coast of Hudson Bay, the inhabitants of the northern forests spoke languages of the Dene, or Athapaskan, family; from the east coast of Hudson Bay to the coast of Labrador, the forest Indians spoke Algonkian languages and named themselves with variations on the word *Innu*. Both Dene and Innu peoples seem to have occupied their homelands for considerable periods, probably for as long as the Palaeo-Eskimos occupied the tundra regions to the north of Indian lands.

In the Barren Grounds to the west of Hudson Bay, sporadic meetings must have occurred over the centuries between the ancestral Dene and the Palaeo-Eskimos, both of whom hunted the migrating caribou herds that are the major animal resource of the region. Indeed, as we saw in an earlier chapter, Palaeo-Eskimos seem to have replaced Dene across the entire Barren Grounds region for a period of several centuries prior to 1000 BC. Yet archaeology has given no hints that these contacts involved the transfer of ideas, materials, or people. Relationships may have been implacably hostile, as they seem to have been between the Chipewyan Indians and the Inuit who occupied this region at the time of Samuel Hearne's eighteenth-century tour of the Barren Grounds. With the development of Dorset culture there is even less likelihood of significant relationships across this ethnic border, since Dorset people seem to have completely withdrawn from the interior and the more southerly coasts adjacent to the tree line.

To the east of Hudson Bay, on the Ungava Peninsula and along the coast of Labrador, there is slightly more evidence for contact and even for the development of trade and exchange of ideas. Before the earliest Palaeo-Eskimos moved south into Labrador, the coastal regions had been occupied by Indian groups known to archaeology as the Maritime Archaic tradition. As early as 7,000 years ago these coastal hunters were erecting burial mounds, and over the following millennia they expended a remarkable amount of energy and artistry in the ceremonial activities that left archaeological traces in their burials. We think of these people as coastal hunters using harpoons and lances with finely polished stone points, probably launched from large dug-out canoes, to hunt sea mammals as large as walrus. At some time around 2000 BC the coastal Indians of northern Labrador encountered the first Palaeo-Eskimo migrants from the north, and over the following 2,000 years the two groups shared the region in some way that is very unclear to archaeologists.

The first hint of contact is the appearance of small chipped-stone arrow points in northern Indian sites, resembling poorly made versions of the exquisitely formed arrow points used by Palaeo-Eskimos. James Tuck, whose work at Saglek Bay first recovered these specimens, has suggested that they may mark the transfer of bow and arrow technology from the Palaeo-Eskimos, whose ancestors had brought it from Siberia, to the Indians of the Americas. The expansion of bow and arrow technology throughout the New World seems consistent with an introduction of about this date, and the early Palaeo-Eskimos may have provided the link between Eurasia and America that effected the introduction. The northern coast of Labrador, where archaeological evidence shows an overlap of Indian and Palaeo-Eskimo occupation zones, would have been a particularly likely area for transfer to occur.

Later evidence of contact between Palaeo-Eskimos and Maritime Archaic Indians comes primarily from the distribution of tools chipped from a unique type of stone. This grey, translucent material is only found in the vicinity of Ramah Bay on the northern Labrador coast, where it occurs in large uniform slabs from which stoneworkers could easily chip finely shaped and attractive weapon points and cutting blades. So appealing was this material that from its discovery at some time before 2000 BC it was widely traded throughout the Indian nations of northeastern North America. Tools made from Ramah chalcedony have been found across the Maritime provinces and New England and as far west as Ontario. Interestingly, over much of the period when this long-distance trade occurred, the Ramah quarries lay within the portion of northern Labrador occupied by Palaeo-Eskimos. The Labrador Indians who traded it southward must have acquired the chalcedony either through frequent expeditions deep into hostile territory or through trade with the Palaeo-Eskimos who owned the quarries. The amount of Ramah stone used by Indian stoneworkers in northeastern North America can probably be measured in tons, suggesting the likelihood of an established trade between Palaeo-Eskimo quarry owners and Indian entrepreneurs over a period of several centuries.

One rather intriguing piece of evidence suggests that this trade continued until very close to the end of the Palaeo-Eskimo occupation of Labrador. This is a small copper coin, minted in Norway during the late eleventh century AD and excavated from an Indian village site in Maine. The discovery of the Maine Penny and its identification as a pre-

Columbian Norse artifact stimulated further excavations in the hope of recovering indications of an early Norse presence in New England. No other objects of European origin were recovered, but the excavations did produce a number of artifacts chipped from Ramah chalcedony, as well as a small fragment of a polished flint 'burin-like tool,' a very characteristic Dorset culture artifact. The evidence hints that the Norse coin had not been brought to the coast of Maine on a Norse ship but had more likely been traded southward with the Ramah stone and the Dorset culture artifact from an initial contact between the Norse and Dorset Palaeo-Eskimos at some location in the eastern Arctic.

Norse Greenlanders

When the outcast Eirik the Red reached Greenland around AD 982, he reported that the island was not occupied but that his crew found traces of earlier inhabitants in the form of stone tools and fragments of skin boats. These remains probably relate to the archaeologically known occupation of southwestern Greenland by Dorset Palaeo-Eskimos, but this occupation had apparently ended before the Norse reached the island.

Dorset people may have continued to live in other parts of Greenland, and a possible meeting between Norse and Palaeo-Eskimos along the forbidding eastern coast of the island is suggested by the story of Thorgils Orrabeinsfostre. He and his crew were shipwrecked on this coast at some time around AD 1000 and had numerous strange and harrowing adventures. The saga is generally considered unreliable as a historical source, but two of the stories hint at a meeting between the shipwrecked crew and an aboriginal population of the area. One relates that the starving Norse saw two witches cutting up a sea mammal beside a hole in the ice, chased them away, and took the animal for themselves. On another occasion, the ship's boat disappeared and was returned by two witches. It is possible that the witches of these stories were a remnant of the last Dorset Palaeo-Eskimo population of Greenland, surviving on the isolated eastern coast after their kin to the west had abandoned the country.

Contacts such as this, however, cannot have had significant influence on either the Norse or the Dorset people. More extensive contacts, which could have led to a sporadic trading relationship, may have developed along the coasts of Labrador and perhaps Baffin Island. We know

The Dorset people came into contact with the Norse who established colonies in western Greenland, and who explored the eastern fringes of Arctic Canada. This photograph shows the reconstruction of the settlement that the Norse attempted at L'Anse aux Meadows, on the northern tip of Newfoundland.

that the Norse began coasting these shores as early as about AD 1000 in order to explore and exploit the regions known as Markland and Vinland. The Markland, or Forest Land, of the Norse sagas can be identified with the forested coasts of Labrador, while Vinland most likely referred to the general area of Newfoundland and the Gulf of St. Lawrence. Voyages to Markland continued until at least 1347, when an Icelandic annal refers to a ship from Markland being driven to Iceland by a storm. It seems likely that Norse visits to Labrador for over three centuries were primarily aimed at obtaining timber for construction of their houses, boats, and other tools, and that their main contacts would have been with Indian inhabitants of the forested portions of the coast. Nevertheless, in order to reach the forests they travelled along the tundra coasts of northern Labrador, occupied by Dorset Palaeo-Eskimos. Small pieces of smelted sheet copper have been recovered from two Dorset sites in the region, one on Hudson Strait and the other on the southeastern coast of Hudson Bay, while the Maine Penny described earlier may have passed through Dorset hands. These scraps of evidence might relate to nothing more than a single hostile encounter between a Dorset hunting band and the crew of a Norse ship's boat surprised during a shore visit. The wide distribution of the evidence, however, suggests a somewhat more intensive relationship between the two peoples.

The End of Isolation

We will probably never know whether the Dorset inhabitants of the eastern Arctic occasionally traded walrus tusks and bearskins for Norse metal goods, brought ashore by wary and well-armed men from small ships coasting south to the Labrador forests. Yet the Dorset people must have known of the Norse, known that another kind of human had appeared off the coasts of their homelands and probably known that dealing with the newcomers could be both profitable and dangerous. They must have long known the same about the Indians who occupied the forests to the south, with whom they seem to have established a means of sharing the country and its resources.

Neither the forest Indians nor the Norse in the eastern seas would effect much change in the way of life that the Palaeo-Eskimos had built for themselves. Both groups had cultures and economies that found little use in the tundra landscape and frozen seas of Arctic Canada. Their relations with the Dorset people were probably limited to sporadic trade when it was mutually beneficial or occasional hostile skirmishes when it was not.

In the centuries after AD 1000, however, a new and much more dangerous threat to the Dorset way of life became apparent. This period saw an expansion of Inuit groups from the large Thule culture whaling towns of the North Alaskan coast. Unlike Norse and Indians, the Inuit saw Arctic Canada as a desirable environment in which to establish their own society. Moreover, the Inuit economy was based on a significantly more efficient technology than that of the Palaeo-Eskimos. The successful capture of a single bowhead whale could provide a winter's supply of meat and oil for a larger community than could be supported by most Dorset hunting bands. The dogsled and the *umiak,* an open, skin-covered boat that could carry twenty or more people, allowed Inuit groups to explore large stretches of new country rapidly and to exploit hunting opportunities over a wide area. The Mongol-type of recurved bow powered by a thick cable of twisted sinew, recently introduced to Alaska along with slat armour of an Asiatic pattern, gave the Inuit a weapon that could be used against alien humans as well as against animal prey. When ancestral Inuit began to move east along the coasts of Amundsen Gulf and penetrate the Dorset homelands, the three millennia of Palaeo-Eskimo isolation came to an end.

CHAPTER 11

The End of the Dorset World

The centuries leading up to AD 1000 brought many changes to the world of the Palaeo-Eskimos. After a thousand years of relative stability both the Dorset people's environment and their human neighbours began to act in unexpected ways.

The environmental change was related to a global warming that affected most of the northern hemisphere late in the first millennium AD, culminating in the conditions known in Europe as the Mediaeval Warm Period. European winters were significantly milder than they had been in earlier times, warmth-loving crops such as grapes were grown much farther north than they are today, and agricultural productivity increased throughout northern Europe. These conditions promoted the population growth and economic advances that marked the development of mediaeval civilization, while in Scandinavia it is thought that the warmer and more productive environment had a hand in the remarkable developments of the Viking Age.

A similar warming trend in Arctic North America, beginning around AD 600 or 700 and lasting for 500 or more years, is evidenced in the ice cores of Greenland, changes in the accumulation of pollen in Arctic lakes and bogs, and other indicators of past climates. We do not know precisely how these changes would have affected Arctic North America. Pollen analysis and the remains of old tree stumps on the tundra testify that the tree line in the Barren Grounds was up to a hundred kilometres north of its present position. This must have influenced the migration patterns of caribou and probably the distribution of other tundra animals. The greatest effect, however, and the one that leaves little in the palaeo-environmental record, must have been in the extent and seasonal duration of sea ice. Slightly milder winters, warmer summers, and shifts in the direction of surface winds must have produced sudden, unpredictable changes in sea ice distribution. Distributions of seals and whales, whose ways of life were closely tied to sea ice conditions, must have also altered in seemingly erratic ways.

For Dorset hunters, the new conditions must have brought a baffling mixture of dangers and opportunities. Over a period of a lifetime, or even over a few years, an area that had rarely known caribou may have become a summer home to tens of thousands of the animals. An ice-covered strait, which for generations had always provided a dependable winter hunting platform, may have failed to freeze until local hunters and their families starved or moved elsewhere in a desperate search for food. Walrus herds that had been concentrated in winter polynia, where they were very vulnerable to ice-edge hunters, may have dispersed into expanded areas of open water and become much more difficult to approach and hunt. People living along coasts that had previously been frozen for most of the year may have suddenly found themselves watching parades of walrus, narwhal, and beluga migrating through the open waters of early summer.

Over a thousand years earlier, as we saw, a changing climate seems to have stimulated the development of the Dorset culture. At that time the climate had been cooling rather than warming, but for the Palaeo-Eskimos the most significant factor must have been the unpredictability of the new conditions. Similar levels of uncertainty can be expected to have occurred with a warming climate and may have stimulated a similar series of cultural and social responses: starvation conditions among small communities, forcing members to move in order to find new sources of food or to seek help from neighbouring bands. Earlier we surmised that the effect of such disruptions – the accumulation of many small-scale family disasters – would appear archaeologically as the breakdown of distinctive local cultures and the appearance of uniform artifact styles over broad areas. Such an archaeological signal did accompany the cooling climates of the early first millennium BC, and a similar pattern appears in the centuries of warming before AD 1000.

According to Inuit tradition, the Tunit furnished the rivers with fish weirs such as
this one used during the early twentieth
century.

The Late Dorset Period

Most of the Dorset artifacts that came to the attention of early archaeologists were, we now recognize, collected from sites occupied during the last few centuries of the culture's existence. In fact, despite the predilection of archaeologists for older materials, and despite a conscious effort to learn more about the early periods of Dorset culture, our largest collections still relate to the phase known to archaeology as Late Dorset. This reflects the Dorset occupation of more – and more widely distributed – sites during their final centuries of existence.

The one region that appears to have been abandoned throughout the Late Dorset period was Newfoundland and the adjacent forested coasts of southern and central Labrador. These areas, which had been a major centre of Palaeo-Eskimo occupation during earlier times, now seem to have been occupied by Indian groups. It is tempting to see the replacement of populations as the result of a warming climate and reduced sea ice, to which the Dorset adaptation might have been especially vulnerable. Yet while such conditions might have made the sub-Arctic adaptations of Indian peoples more competitive than those of the Palaeo-Eskimos, we should remember that the Dorset people had successfully lived under sub-Arctic conditions for a millennium or more, and probably could have adapted to a warmer climate and the changes in animal distributions that it produced. Although we can only speculate on the reasons, we know that the Dorset people abandoned the forested coasts of Newfoundland and Labrador shortly after AD 500.

This one instance of territorial retreat, however, is more than matched by a major expansion on the western and northern fringes of the Dorset world. Late Dorset sites are found as far west as the western coast of Victoria Island and on the adjacent mainland coast of Dolphin and Union Strait. Late Dorset village sites appear across the High Arctic islands to the north of Parry Channel, a huge area that had apparently been abandoned for many centuries, since very early in Dorset times. Late Dorset people also seem to have crossed to northern Greenland and moved south to occupy the fiords along the southwestern coasts of that country. The territory occupied by Dorset people reached its maximum extent during the Late Dorset period.

As striking as the expansion of Dorset occupation across great areas of previously unoccupied land is the remarkable uniformity of the artifacts from their settlements. From northern Labrador to Victoria Island and to Greenland, the makers of tools and weapons followed identical patterns and took pains to ensure that their manufactures conformed closely. The homogeneity is most marked in the Late Dorset period and, as suggested earlier, must have resulted from wide-ranging networks of local communication combined with occasional long-distance travel, probably associated with trade or the acquisition of rare and precious raw materials. It was also suggested that the Dorset people perhaps ascribed mystical qualities to these exotic materials and that their trade may have been associated with the spread and consolidation of a system of magico-religious beliefs. Certainly in the Late Dorset period the uniformity of style is associated with a massive increase in the amount of artistic activity, as measured by the large numbers of carvings recovered from Late Dorset villages. Is it possible that both the amount and the uniformity of art production are associated with a new material that appears throughout the Late Dorset world: meteoritic iron?

An Arctic Iron Age?

When nineteenth-century European explorers penetrated the homelands of the Polar Inuit in the Thule district of far northwestern Greenland, they found this small and isolated group using tools with sharp-edged iron blades. These tools were fashioned from a local source: a group of large iron meteorites clustered in a valley near Cape York. The meteorites had long been known to the local Inuit population, and small fragments of iron had been widely traded across Arctic Canada since the first Inuit arrived almost 1,000 years ago. It seems likely that ancestral Inuit learned of this extremely rare and valuable resource from their Dorset predecessors, and it has been suggested that knowledge of the iron source was a factor in attracting the Inuit eastward from their Alaskan home.

Iron must have been a prized commodity for the Palaeo-Eskimos who first discovered the large strange-looking boulders that now lie in museums in New York and Copenhagen. The high nickel content of meteoritic iron makes it much harder than ordinary smelted iron and more difficult to work. Yet small flakes of iron could be removed from the meteorites by pounding them with heavy rocks; these flakes could then be flattened and shaped by cold-hammering and ground against sandstone to form a keen and long-lasting edge. To craftworkers who spent a significant part of their lives in carving artifacts from hard bone, ivory, or antler, the possession of iron-bladed tools was a great boon. The material must have been more highly prized since it all derived from a single locality – the only source on earth, to the knowledge of the Palaeo-Eskimos.

The significance of the iron source may have been augmented if the meteorites suddenly appeared in a valley that was previously known. We do not know when the Cape York meteorites fell from the sky, but it seems likely that many of them fell onto the Greenlandic icecap and reached their final resting place by melting from the edge of the glacier that had carried them down toward the coast. It is therefore unlikely that Palaeo-Eskimos saw the brilliant shower of falling stars that brought these large meteorites to earth, but they may have discovered them newly released from the glacier.

The discovery seems to have occurred near the beginning of the Late Dorset period, since no specimens are known from earlier Palaeo-Eskimo settlements. In contrast, Late Dorset settlements across the Arctic have produced either small iron blades or iron oxide stains in the sockets of bone or antler tools. There seems to have been a coincidental increase in the use of native copper, from the Coppermine River and Victoria Island sources long known to Palaeo-Eskimo traders and artisans. Perhaps the use of iron tools stimulated the value and trade of this similar but softer and more easily worked material. The sudden growth in the number of carvings produced during the Late Dorset period is usually ascribed to social or religious factors, but we should keep in mind that the widespread availability of iron and native copper may have contributed to, or at least facilitated, this phenomenon.

An Artistic Florescence

A great majority of the specimens listed in museum catalogues as Dorset art came from settlements occupied late in the history of the culture. Several kinds of artifacts – the antler wands covered with carved faces, the bell-like containers fashioned in the form of paired walrus, the tubes with opposed heads of caribou and wolf, the tiny spatulas with animal-head handles, flat perforated plaques in the form of stylized bears – seem to have been made and used only during this period. Other classes, such as miniature weapons and naturalistic sculptures of animals, were carved with increasing frequency. In some sites, the artifacts classed as art are more numerous than any other category, even such utilitarian and economically important artifacts as harpoon heads, knife handles, and skin scrapers.

The function of art is often, and probably naïvely, considered to be 'decoration' or 'enhancement of life.' From such a viewpoint, art flourishes in cultures that have mastered the economic basis of their survival and can afford to spend time and effort in developing enhancements. The surge of carving activity during the final centuries of Dorset culture might be partly explained by such an argument. It occurred, after all, in a period of warming climate, when the Dorset population spread out to occupy more regions of the Arctic than at any earlier time. But any simple argument linking an increase in artistic activity to the warming climate is probably mistaken. As pointed out earlier, the primary effect of any climatically driven environmental change – whether its long-term results were positive or negative – must have been unpredictability in local environments and a consequent hardship for local hunting populations.

Artistic florescence in a time of uncertainty suggests a different dynamic from one that occurs during a period of affluence and security. It suggests that 'Dorset art' was not made simply for decoration or amusement but for protection or as an aid in coping with an environment in which the rules were suddenly changing. The interpretation of Dorset art as a phenomenon intimately associated with religion, magic, and a shamanistic view of the universe and its powers is consistent with a response to environmental uncertainty and economic insecurity.

In the spring of 1923, the ethnologist Knud Rasmussen arrived in the country of the Netsilingmiut, a small band of Inuit who occupied one of the most impoverished regions of the central Arctic. For the past century or more the ancestors of the Netsilingmiut had dealt with the deteriorating climate and uncertain environment of the Little Ice Age. At the same time, although very few Europeans penetrated the Netsilik country, the area was swept by rumours of a changed world, a growing stream of European artifacts, and almost certainly by diseases of European origin. Rasmussen was impressed by the Netsilik's tales of famine and disaster and by their fear of their environment. In order to cope with the situation, the Netsilik more than any other Inuit group depended on large numbers of personal amulets, representations of the creatures whose spirits could be invoked in times of need. One small boy carried eighty amulets attached to his clothing. The Netsilik reported that in earlier times a person had needed only one amulet but that both the powers of amulets and the powers of shamans had declined in their present world.

It is inviting to see a similar situation as the cause of the great increase in carved amulets and shamanistic implements during the final phase of the Dorset culture. The Late Dorset people inherited an ancient religious system and world view that saw personal spirit helpers as the medium through which humans could control, or at least manipulate, the small-scale events of their environment. Facing an environment that was no longer behaving in predictable ways and the appearance of unknown peoples, first along the fringes of their country and eventually in its very heart, the religion of the Dorset people and its associated amulets and tools must have acquired a new importance.

Longhouse Builders

Our picture of Palaeo-Eskimo society is sketched from remarkably little evidence. Most is in the form of assumptions derived from the size of their occupation sites and the apparent duration of occupations at these settlements. In the Late Dorset period this sort of evidence becomes more abundant and more varied but is no easier to interpret.

Many Dorset settlement sites, especially those in the environmentally rich eastern Arctic areas that saw the densest Palaeo-Eskimo occupation, are places where people lived for generation after generation while exploiting a stable but localized concentration of animals. The archaeological remains of such settlements are dense layers of artifacts and bones, house sites that have been used time and again or dismantled for their materials by later occupants. They are very difficult to understand. On the fringes of Dorset territory however, on the barren islands of the High Arctic or along the more southerly coasts of Hudson Bay and Labrador, the remains of Dorset communities are more clearly preserved. And in these areas, almost all Late Dorset sites look remarkably similar: a line of four or five dwellings behind a thin scatter of midden that usually represents the accumulated garbage of a few weeks or a few seasons. The number of dwellings is remarkably constant, suggesting that through most of the year the Dorset people preferred to live in small communities of perhaps twenty to thirty people, all of whom were probably close kin. A contemporary Inuit camp group consisting of an elderly couple and two or

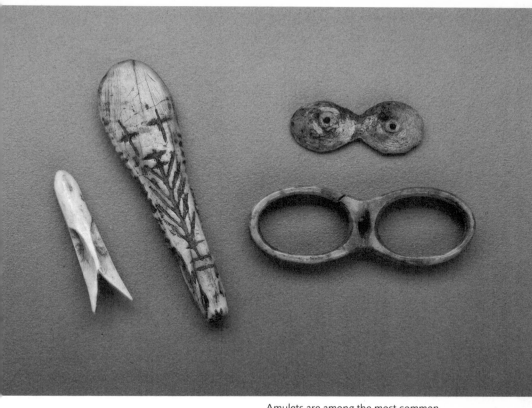

Amulets are among the most common objects recovered from Late Dorset settlements. Although the meaning behind these objects is obscure, they appear in identical styles from widely separated areas of the Dorset world.

three of their grown children with their families could probably serve as the model for a typical Dorset settlement.

Settlements of this size seem to have been occupied both in summer and in winter. The individual dwellings in such settlements are of two types, which usually do not occur together on the same site. One is a shallow rectangular pit, ten to twenty centimetres deep and roughly three by four metres on the sides, with rounded corners and surrounded by a low mound of earth or gravel. The interiors of such pits have a thin sprinkling of artifacts and bone fragments but no evidence of hearths or other structures. These seem to be the remains of summer tents: small, skin-covered structures supported by driftwood poles, the skirts of the tent weighted with the gravel and earth dug from the interior of the dwelling. When the tent was removed, the spilled earth formed the characteristic ring around these structures. There is usually no evidence that a fire was built or that lamps were used in these tents, and they were probably shelters from wind and rain during the warmer seasons of the year, perhaps occupied between about May and September.

The other type of dwelling is about the same size – four by five metres and occasionally somewhat larger – but more complex. These structures are centred on a midpassage formed from rock slabs or boulders, usually about a metre wide and running lengthwise through the centre of the structure. The floors of these passages are paved with slabs, the edges marked by vertical stones; they are interrupted by one or two hearths marked by vertically placed and braced pot rests, which would have supported small soapstone vessels. The living and sleeping areas to the sides of the central passage are usually unpaved gravel or earth. One village on tiny Dundas Island was hidden for most or all of the year beneath a large snowbank; when the snow melted back in an unusually warm August, the houses were so well preserved that moss and willow bedding materials still lined the floor areas on either side of the passages. These structures were probably the foundations of dwellings occupied during the colder portions of the year. The absence of a ring of boulders or earth that would have held down the skirts of a tent suggests that the houses were built of snow, either of stacked blocks or more likely of snow piled against the walls of a tent to hold down the skirts. Occasionally, in the more southerly areas of Dorset occupation, these structures were dug as much as fifty centimetres into the ground and may have had walls of piled turf blocks.

Given the importance of winter shelter under Arctic conditions, ingenuity and the use of local building resources must have led to a wide variety of winter dwellings.

A third type of building constructed by the Late Dorset people has led to much conjecture. Dorset 'longhouses' were elongated rectangular structures outlined by large boulders or vertically braced slabs of rock. Most are six to seven metres wide, and they range in length from ten to forty-five metres. The walls are generally about one metre high and seem to have served a symbolic rather than a protective purpose. In fact, Dorset longhouses might be better thought of as enclosures than as houses. Such large structures cannot have been roofed with the materials available to Dorset communities, and there is no indication that they were covered. Nor is there evidence of cooking or heating fires in most longhouses, although there is a sufficient scatter of animal bones and broken artifacts to suggest that people did live in them for at least short periods. Perhaps the tents of individual families were set up within the enclosures, which provided a symbolic boundary to mark the communal ties of local bands that joined together for a portion of their annual cycle.

The preparation of food also seems to have been a communal activity at longhouse settlements. Rows of cooking hearths are found outside the enclosures, often built into a long line paved with slabs. Sometimes these rows are built directly against an exterior wall of the longhouse, and sometimes the hearths are at some distance from the main structure but in a line equal in length to the enclosure.

Only a few Dorset longhouses have been found, but their wide distribution – from Victoria Island in the west to northern Québec and northward to Ellesmere Island – indicates that these mysterious structures were a basic feature of Late Dorset culture and social practice. They are invariably found at locations that provide a rich source of food during a part of the summer: a run of fish, a herd of caribou, nesting seabirds, or a concentration of sea mammals in a small polynia. Such a resource would have provided the opportunity for several local bands to join together for perhaps a few days or even a few weeks in order to trade materials and news, to meet old friends, to arrange marriages and mourn deaths, and to break the monotony of life in small and isolated social groups. The summer longhouse meetings must have been festive occasions, enhanced by the sense of security provided by a large number of acquaintances and an

The remains of a Dorset longhouse, over thirty metres in length, lie on the coast of Victoria Island, at the western limit of Dorset occupation.

assured supply of food. They must also have been a time for contests, dances, performances, and religious activities, celebrations of the solidarity and cultural similarity that bound the local bands into a community. These meetings must have provided the main mechanism for the spread of stylistic changes throughout the population and for the remarkable uniformity of Late Dorset culture. As places of communal celebration, or perhaps as places where local bands could assemble in times of crisis, the huge structures that dot the beaches of Arctic Canada must have been powerful symbols in the cultures of small communities.

It is not clear just how or when the Dorset people developed the idea of building them. When they were first discovered in Arctic Québec, Dorset longhouses were mistakenly identified as the remains of a mediaeval Norse occupation. Others have suggested that Greenlandic Norse structures may have served as a prototype for those of the Dorset people, but it is now certain that Dorset builders began to construct longhouses some centuries earlier than the Norse occupation of Greenland. The Cree and other Indian peoples of the northeastern forest also built large and temporary ceremonial structures, using brush and skins, and these have been suggested as possible models for Dorset longhouses as well. Or perhaps the concept of a communal enclosure was simply developed by the Dorset people themselves, and the idea spread throughout the population as did so many other elements of culture, technology, and art.

The ruins of Dorset longhouse enclosures are among the most impressive archaeological remains in Arctic regions. They lie abandoned on isolated beaches, their rows of cooking hearths washed clean of charcoal and ash, surrounded by scatters of animal bones and tiny carvings. It is easy to imagine such structures serving as the focus for the final act in the history of the Palaeo-Eskimos.

Disappearance of the Tunit

The archaeological puzzle of the end of Dorset culture is far from being solved. There is no evidence to suggest the dwindling of a small and meagre group with only a tenuous hold on their environment. Rather, the Dorsets disappeared from history at a time when they were building longhouse enclosures across the Arctic, often in areas that had not been occupied for centuries or millennia. Their sites were full of carvings, each of them representing great care, skill, and purpose. Whatever happened to them seems to have occurred suddenly and to have left almost no trace in the archaeological record. When we reconstruct these events, we do so on the basis of a few scattered accounts from the oral history of the Inuit. The archaeological evidence shows only that Dorset culture was replaced across Arctic Canada and Greenland by the culture of the ancestral Inuit who moved east from Alaska about 1,000 years ago.

The historical traditions of the central Arctic Inuit tell of a people named Tunit who occupied the country before them. As we saw earlier, they are usually portrayed as large and strong people but peaceful, timid, and easily put to flight. It was the Tunit who made the country habitable by locating the places where caribou herds concentrated at a river cross- ing and building the lines of boulder cairns to guide the animals to an ambush. They also built the boulder fish weirs that made it possible to spear char during their summer runs up Arctic rivers. They are said to have been great workers in stone, to have dressed in bearskins, and to have used tiny stone lamps, which they placed beneath their parkas while waiting for seals.

Some stories tell of Inuit and Tunit communities living in harmony and even of hunting together. In contrast to the historical traditions deal- ing with Indians, there are very few accounts of attacks by Tunit on the settlements of the Inuit. Most of the traditions tell of eventual Inuit attacks on the Tunit, however, and the accounts always end with the Tunit being chased from their homelands and disappearing forever. Typical is the story told to Knud Rasmussen in 1922 by the Igloolik historian Ivaluardjuk:

> The Tunit were a strong people, and yet they were driven from their villages by others who were more numerous, by many people of great ancestors; but so greatly did they love their country, that when they were leaving Uglit, there was a man who, out of desperate love for his village, struck the rocks with his harpoon and made the stones fly about like bits of ice.

Can the legendary Tunit be identified with the archaeologists' Dorset people? Both the Tunit and the Dorsets were somewhat like the Inuit but were also different in many significant ways. Both Tunit and Dorsets inhabited Arctic Canada when the Inuit arrived and both disap- peared shortly after that event. There seems to be little doubt that the Tunit legends are historical accounts referring to the final generations of

Stone fox traps such as this hollow structure, which the fox enters from the top,
may be a Tunit style that continued to be
used by the Inuit.

the Palaeo-Eskimos, and these accounts are probably our most reliable source in searching for explanations of how Palaeo-Eskimo culture came to an end.

The Village at Brooman Point

One is tempted to think in terms of the Tunit legends while trying to interpret the archaeological remains of Late Dorset and early Inuit settlements in Arctic Canada. A decade ago I was faced with such a problem in excavating and trying to understand an early Inuit village in the High Arctic. At the southern end of Brooman Point, a barren spit extending from the eastern coast of Bathurst Island, lie the remains of twenty large winter houses built from boulders, turf, and whale bones. These houses were built by the Thule culture Inuit, probably at some time around AD 1100, and they seem to represent the first appearance of Inuit in this region of the Arctic. They were obviously attracted to this location by the sea mammals that concentrated in a small polynia adjacent to the site, an area of open water that remains unfrozen for most or all of the winter because of tidal currents sweeping around the tip of Brooman Point. Walrus and seals now winter in this polynia, and in earlier times it may have served as an early-summer home for migrating whales; the bones of at least twenty large bowhead whales were used in building the Thule winter houses at Brooman Point, and bones of smaller whales were found among the food refuse of the village. The deep middens of animal bones surrounding the winter houses indicate that the Inuit who lived here had bountiful supplies of meat and of sea mammal oil for their lamps.

The early Inuit were not the first hunters to be attracted by the polynia off Brooman Point. The raised beaches behind the Thule village are dotted with numerous small patches of vegetation and broken slabs of rock, marking the remains of camps occupied by the Palaeo-Eskimos who began to visit the area about 4,000 years ago and who returned sporadically until the arrival of the Inuit. The final Palaeo-Eskimo occupation is represented by the remains of several Late Dorset summer tent pits scattered around the houses of the Inuit village, as well as by the remains of a longhouse sheltered behind a small bluff a few hundred metres from the village. It seems likely that the main part of the Late Dorset settlement lay directly beneath the houses of the Thule village, as Dorset culture artifacts are found throughout the turf and gravel that was dug up to insulate the

The open water of the Mediaeval Warm
Period may have had a hand in the disappearance of the Dorset people. The tip of
Brooman Point, on Bathurst Island, bears
the remains of a Late Dorset settlement
and a very early Thule Inuit village, both
probably dating to around AD 1200.

Whale bones, used as the walls and rafters of winter houses, mark the remains of an early Inuit winter village in Arctic Canada. The wealth of the Inuit economy is epitomized by a comparison of a site such as this with the meagre remains of a Dorset village.

walls of the Thule houses. It is not unusual to find Dorset artifacts in the walls of Thule Inuit houses. Not only were the two groups attracted to similar settlement sites, but the early Inuit were probably also attracted by the turf that was nourished by the remains of earlier Dorset occupation and provided good building material. But at Brooman Point there were indications that the two occupations came very close together in time and could represent a case of direct contact between the two populations.

In normal circumstances, lost artifacts lying on the surface or in the shallow soil of Dorset villages soon acquire a patina of soil stain, or the crackled surface of ivory that is exposed to the freeze-thaw cycles of Arctic weather, or the mazes of etched lines produced by the roots of small plants. In comparison, the artifacts abandoned by Thule culture Inuit in the interiors of their winter houses are soon frozen into the well-insulated soil beneath the fallen turfs and whale bones of a collapsed roof. When excavated from the permafrost several centuries later, they look as if they had been laid aside by their owners only yesterday. Most of the Dorset artifacts found in the Thule houses at Brooman Point were remarkably well preserved, as if they had been incorporated into the permanently frozen soil of Thule house walls almost immediately after they had been made. So complete was the preservation that one harpoon head was still attached to a leather thong and another still retained a lashing of fragile sinew. A tiny basket woven from plant roots and containing a few Dorset artifacts is the only known example of basketry preserved in a Dorset site (Plate 16). These finds seem to indicate that the Thule winter houses must have been built on Brooman Point very shortly after the Dorset settlement had been abandoned, perhaps even in the same season.

That the last Dorset occupants of the site already knew of the Thule Inuit is suggested by a single Thule artifact – the bone handle of a knife – found buried in the floor of one of the small Late Dorset tent pits located at some distance from the main village. This artifact seems to have been left by the Dorset occupants of the tent, who may have obtained it from an Inuk or perhaps scavenged it from a Thule site somewhere in the region. Other than this hint of direct contact, however, there is no indication that the Dorset Palaeo-Eskimos and the Thule Inuit at Brooman Point ever met, traded tools or materials, or learned from the other's technology.

The archaeological remains from Brooman Point may bear witness

The remains of the Late Dorset longhouse
at Brooman Point. The early Inuit occupants
of the site have removed the portion in the
foreground to build a large boulder cache.

to a series of small-scale events much like those described in some accounts of the meetings between Inuit and Tunit. The first rumours of alien invaders probably spread in early summer, when the local Dorset bands assembled at the longhouse enclosure for their annual gathering. During the spring a hunter working his way through the ice fields to the south, perhaps hunting newborn seals in their dens among the pressure-ridges of sea ice pushed up by the movement of the tides and wind in Barrow Strait, may have crossed the tracks of a strange sled that was much larger than those used by the Dorsets. Another group may have come upon an abandoned camp along the southern shore of Bathurst Island, the tent foundation arranged in a strange manner that no Palaeo-Eskimo would think of using. Perhaps they even collected a broken knife handle that had been left behind by the people who made the camp.

Discoveries such as these must have been worrisome omens in the lives of an isolated society. No family would want to be on its own when it encountered alien and perhaps non-human strangers, and the longhouse assembly may have been extended as long as possible into the summer. Amulets may have been refurbished with power and new ones carved representing spirits that might help protect the small community against the unknown forces that were appearing in the country. Some of these specimens may have contributed to the extremely large number of carvings that were incorporated into the walls of Thule houses and later recovered by archaeologists.

The actual encounter that resulted in Brooman Point permanently changing hands could have occurred in many ways. The Dorset community may have wakened one night to the barking of dogs, the splash of paddles, and voices talking in a strange language from a fogbank lying just off shore. A shift in the wind could have revealed a travelling party of Inuit, women and children and dogs in a huge skin-covered boat surrounded by a scattered flock of a dozen hunters in kayaks. The mutual surprise of the two groups probably prevented any immediate hostilities, and we can imagine the Inuit hastening away and out of sight, perhaps behind an offshore island. But in their glimpse of Brooman Point they could not have missed that they had discovered a particularly favoured oasis in a barren countryside. The beaches would have been littered with the bones of sea mammals captured by Dorset hunters, and the grinding sweep of pack ice around the point would have been the telltale sign of tidal currents that promised a long season of open water and a concentration of animals.

We do not know what drew small groups of Inuit east across Arctic Canada: whether they were searching for new and unexploited hunting territories, hoping for wealth by gaining access to the sources of native copper and meteoritic iron that had spread across the Arctic through Palaeo-Eskimo trade routes, or simply fleeing hostilities flaring among the relatively dense Inuit populations of the western Arctic. Whatever their purpose, an Inuit exploration party reaching Bathurst Island from the Amundsen Gulf region far to the west, an area that had been home to Inuit for the past century or two, would have had to traverse almost a thousand kilometres of barren and ice-choked straits. Chancing across the Brooman Point polynia, they could not have afforded to neglect such evidence of economic security after passing through and perhaps barely surviving so much worthless and dangerous territory.

The two communities probably scouted each other for days, watching from hilltops and from kayaks poised to flee if pursued. Eventually one group – most likely the Inuit, who would have had more experience in meeting strangers – probably decided that a meeting was inevitable. They would have staged such an encounter so as to show themselves at their most formidable and to give themselves the advantage in case a skirmish developed. The Dorsets must have accommodated themselves as best they could to such a meeting, and each group would have attempted the complex protocol that any society has when encountering unknown and potentially hostile strangers. One group may have laid down their weapons and stood with their hands raised to show themselves harmless; the other may have sent forward an elderly woman to assure the strangers that they were meant no harm. If all went well the groups would eventually have mingled, women and children brought out of hiding and food prepared by the hosts. Over the following hours the prospects for trade would have been investigated, languages compared and a few similar words remarked with joyful recognition, and the younger people would have noticed the attractions of those in the other camp.

Did the longhouse behind the bluff at Brooman Point ever serve as the site for such a feast? If so, how long could such a state of friendship and harmony have lasted? Could it have long survived a mixture of mutual suspicion, incomprehension of the other's languages and customs and motives, and the knowledge that both groups were competing for the

Alaskan Inuit painted during the early nineteenth century. The Thule culture Inuit met
by the Dorset people probably looked
quite similar.

same resources, on which their lives depended? The Tunit stories suggest that peace between the two communities could not have lasted long. It was inevitable that an incident, either serious or relatively trivial, would have unleashed a series of events that would result in one community being banished. One of the legends reports that a misunderstanding over the death of a dog led to the local Tunit fleeing their homeland, and we can imagine any number of similar occurrences that would have led to the same result.

In any hostile encounter, the Inuit newcomers would have been the probable victors. Their transportation technology, including dogsleds and large, skin-covered umiaks for water travel, allowed them to travel in numbers that must have been at least equal to most local Dorset groups. They were equipped with powerful bows, which could be used against humans as well as animals and could be deadly at a much greater range than the spears and harpoons of Dorset hunters. When the recurved bow of Mongol type had been introduced to the ancestral Inuit of Alaska, it appeared in company with slat armour of a pattern used throughout eastern Asia, suggesting that the Inuit who arrived in Arctic Canada came from a culture with a long tradition of intervillage warfare. Such a heritage must have been incomprehensible to the small and scattered family groups of Dorset people, making them even more vulnerable in contact with the newcomers.

Inuit explorers may have brought an even more deadly weapon, which even they did not understand, in the form of diseases to which Palaeo-Eskimo populations had never been exposed. Although the ancestral Inuit of Alaska were relatively isolated from the major disease centres of the tropical and subtropical world, their sporadic dealings across Bering Strait must have brought them into occasional contact with infectious diseases such as influenza, and local epidemics were probably not unknown over the past 2,000 or more years. The introduction of disease pathogens to isolated Dorset populations would most likely have resulted in the same type of 'virgin soil epidemics' that have decimated aboriginal populations over the past few centuries of global travel. It is now recognized that the extreme vulnerability of aboriginal peoples to disease resides largely in the genetic uniformity of such small, isolated populations; viruses transmute themselves so quickly in adaptation to their hosts that they are much more effective against another person who is genetically similar.

An Inuit *umiak* in the eastern Arctic during
the early twentieth century. A sight like
this may have been the first indication that
Dorset people were no longer alone in
their homelands.

The artifacts recovered from an early Inuit
village are based on Alaskan patterns and
technologies, which were much more
efficient than those of the Palaeo-Eskimos.

Given their 3,000 or more years of isolation from other peoples, the Palaeo-Eskimos must have comprised a population of remarkable genetic uniformity and thus would have been extremely vulnerable to new diseases. If illness were associated with the newcomers from the west, it would have been both a powerful cause of hostility and a reason for fleeing from contact with the strangers.

Whatever mixture of causes, precipitated by whatever specific incidents, the results are clear in the archaeology of Brooman Point: the Dorset people abandoned their claim to the site, and the Inuit established a settlement that was to last for at least a generation. The first of a series of heavily insulated winter houses must have been built during the first autumn after the Inuit arrived, over the remains of the Dorset community. Others were added in subsequent years but so quickly that material as fragile as a tiny basket or the sinew binding of a Dorset harpoon had not decomposed before they were incorporated into the house walls.

Few if any Dorset people would have been killed in the episode at Brooman Point. Large-scale killing has rarely been a part of warfare among peoples living in small societies, and there is no reason to think that it had a significant role in the displacement of the Palaeo-Eskimos. Fear of the newcomers – of their weapons, of their magic and perhaps the sickness that it produced, and of their aggressive attitude – would have been equally effective. Inuit legends tell repeatedly that the local Tunit groups fled their homelands and disappeared. It is easy to imagine such a scene at Brooman Point. The Dorset people would have eventually realized that the newcomers were planning to stay in the area, and by this time it would have also become apparent that their amulets and spirit helpers could not protect them against the foreigners. They were helpless against people who could capture animals as large as the huge bowhead whales that had always cruised safely along the coasts inhabited by Palaeo-Eskimos, who could kill from a distance with arrows and magic, and who could afford to treat the Dorset people with contempt. A climax may have been reached when the Dorsets offended Inuit custom in sharing the meat of a captured whale, or when a woman was taken by force to be the wife of an Inuk, or when a Dorset shaman learned from his spirits that only trouble could come from staying among the Inuit.

The departure must have been swift, perhaps in the first darkness of early autumn. The small Dorset tents could be quickly dismantled, their

A kitchen match provides scale for a miniature hearth built of tiny slabs of stone. The
remains of this Dorset child's play house
have survived several centuries after the
disappearance of her people.

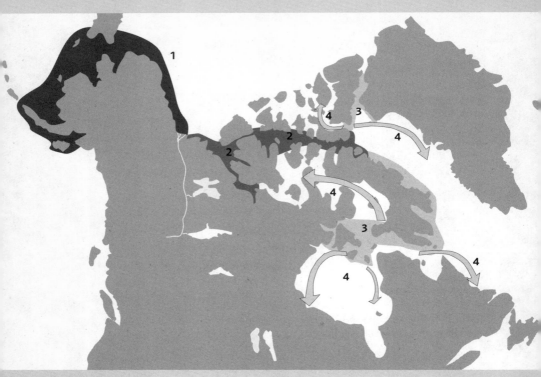

MAP 11.1
Stages in the Inuit invasion of Arctic
Canada. This map attempts to reconstruct
the stages by which ancestral Inuit moved
east from their Alaskan homelands in the
centuries after AD 1000, displacing the earlier Palaeo-Eskimo occupants of Arctic
North America.

Key:
1 Original Inuit homeland
2 Initial eastward push, probably about
   AD 1000
3 Expansion into maritime regions, AD 1000-
   1200?
4 Occupation of remaining areas, AD 1200-
   1500?

boulder weights tumbled about the longhouse enclosure, covering tools and toys and carvings lost in the haste. Belongings quickly gathered, people and dogs loaded with packs of jumbled possessions, hearths were extinguished for the last time at the Brooman Point longhouse. Watched from a distance by their enemies, the small train of people would have begun their trek north, up the barren gravel beaches of Crozier Strait and away from the open water now controlled by Inuit hunters. Along the ice-choked channels to the north lay other hunting areas, not as rich or as dependable as the Brooman Point polynia but not as attractive to the whale-hunting Inuit, whose quarry rarely travelled north from Lancaster Sound. Here they and perhaps their children and grandchildren might be able to live in their traditional manner without fear of invasion. But the Inuit advance was inexorable and eventually put an end to the Palaeo-Eskimo world.

The Inuit Inherit the Arctic

Episodes similar to the one we have imagined for the Brooman Point village must have occurred scores of times in other locations. Our archaeological scale is simply too crude to measure how long it took for this process to run its eventual course. At some Thule culture Inuit sites in the eastern Arctic, the artifacts left behind are so similar to those of Alaska that their makers could not have been much more than a generation removed from their western homelands. In other areas, radiocarbon dates on Late Dorset sites seem to suggest that some Palaeo-Eskimo groups survived for five centuries or more after the first appearance of the Inuit.

The period of displacement probably lay somewhere between these extremes. The Inuit were capable of making extremely rapid advances into areas that provided them with the economic opportunities to which they were accustomed. Their umiaks were able to transport an entire camp group with all its equipment and dogs. Such a group would have been capable of travelling several hundred kilometres during a summer and still establishing a secure winter village at a location where they happened to kill a bowhead whale or a large number of walrus or beluga, or where conditions promised a winter supply of seals or caribou. They would also have been capable of displacing any Dorset community that had traditionally used such a wintering site. Over the next few years they would have explored their surroundings and perhaps made another major move into previously unknown and unexploited waters.

We think that this process brought the Inuit fairly quickly through the inhospitable channels separating Amundsen Gulf from Barrow Strait and Lancaster Sound. Here they would have found themselves among populations of whale, walrus, and seal almost as dense as those of the western Arctic. Following the open water east to where the herds of sea mammals migrated each autumn they would have found even richer hunting grounds around Baffin Bay. Groups moving north would have crossed Smith Sound to Greenland, where they soon encountered the Norse. Those that moved south down the coast of Baffin Island would have been attracted west by the tidal currents of Hudson Strait and into northern Hudson Bay. In any of these areas during the relatively mild climatic conditions of the Mediaeval Warm Period the open-water hunting techniques developed in Alaska would have provided the Inuit with an easy livelihood. All of these coasts could have been explored and lightly occupied within a very few generations.

Throughout this period of exploration and expansion, while Inuit occupation thrust through the heart of Dorset territory and surrounded it on the east, it seems likely that the Dorset people survived in most areas that the Inuit had not reached. The entire High Arctic, north of Lancaster Sound and Baffin Bay, may have remained in Dorset hands, as did the remote regions of the central Arctic south of Lancaster Sound. The Arctic region of Québec and Labrador, protected on the north by the hundred-kilometre unfrozen width of Hudson Strait, seems also to have been a stronghold of Late Dorset occupation. Here are found the most massive remains of longhouse enclosures, as well as huge cairns or beacons, which may have been designed to warn intruders that the land was already occupied. In all of these areas, the Dorsets seem to have maintained an aloof distance from the Inuit, their technology, and their culture. The Dorset settlements that date to this period have yielded large numbers of carvings, as well as artifacts in styles that seem to have been uninfluenced by Inuit technology. Only the occasional appearance of circular holes in artifacts in place of the more characteristic elongated perforations suggests that Dorset craftspeople may have copied the appearance of Thule Inuit artifacts manufactured with bow drills. We may suspect that, like their technology, most of the other patterns of Palaeo-Eskimo life persisted unchanged by contact with the newcomers who had taken over the most productive regions of the Dorset homelands.

After the first century or two, Inuit expansion entered another phase. The populations of areas occupied by the Thule culture Inuit had probably increased significantly, and the Inuit had gained a good deal of knowledge about Arctic Canada and how to exploit its resources. This period also saw a gradual cooling, as the Mediaeval Warm Period came to an end and the Arctic began a slow slide into the cold climates of the sixteenth- to nineteenth-century Little Ice Age. As the Inuit learned to cope with these changing conditions, probably by placing greater reliance on smaller animals – seals, caribou, and fish – than on open-water hunting of large sea mammals, they would have become capable of living in a much wider range of habitats.

Economic adaptation and expansion into areas away from open coasts and the routes of the large whales would have brought the Inuit into direct competition and confrontation with the remaining Dorset populations. Once again the pattern of encounter and retreat must have been repeated time and again. With each retreat into a more inhospitable region, the likelihood of survival through the coming winter must have been less. Small Palaeo-Eskimo groups had always suffered winter hardship and occasional starvation, but the statistical balance in favour of survival must have gradually swung toward the opposite pole.

During the century or two that it took the Inuit to expand into most regions of the Arctic, local Dorset groups must have suffered starvation and death with increasing frequency. By the sixteenth century, when European contact brought a new set of challenges to the Inuit of Arctic Canada and Greenland, the Palaeo-Eskimos and their cultural tradition were effectively extinct. It was the end of the first experiment that humans had made in surviving the far reaches of the Arctic environment. It had lasted for over 3,000 years.

Did the Dorset People Survive?

The extinction of the Dorset culture is clearly visible in the archaeological record. No Dorset sites can be securely dated to the period after about AD 1500, and all of the known sites occupied after this period are clearly settlements of the Thule culture Inuit. There is no blending of the two technological traditions, such as might have occurred if the two groups had gradually merged through a tradition of partnerships, intermarriages, and mutual acculturation. Just as the Dorset settlements of the previous few centuries had shown no evidence that Inuit technology was adopted, the Inuit seem to have ignored most of the technology of their Dorset predecessors. Archaeological evidence totally supports the evidence of Inuit historical tradition: the Tunit fled their homelands and disappeared forever.

But can we interpret this sort of evidence as indicating that the Dorset people became biologically and culturally extinct, leaving no trace of their physical or cultural heritage among the Inuit peoples who took their place across much of Arctic North America? If the society of the Thule culture Inuit was anything like that of their more recent descendants, then it seems very likely that some members of the Dorset population must have been incorporated into the communities of Inuit. Over the generations of contact, there must have been many occasions when a Tunit woman was persuaded or stolen from her family to become the wife of an Inuk and when children were given or taken in adoption. As the Dorset people retreated into poorer and ever poorer territory, some individuals or remnants of small families must have attempted to join themselves to Inuit communities as an alternative to inevitable starvation. Through mechanisms such as these, the Palaeo-Eskimos must have contributed to the biological heritage of the Inuit population, and many of today's Inuit can probably trace a small proportion of their heredity to the Tunit.

The cultural survival of the Palaeo-Eskimo tradition is a different question, and one that is more difficult to answer. A number of suggestions have been made concerning the Palaeo-Eskimo origins of certain aspects of Inuit culture and technology. The domed snow house is one of the more intriguing possibilities. Long snow knives made from antler or ivory, very similar to those used by the later Inuit for cutting snow blocks, are known from some Dorset sites. These tools provide evidence supporting the idea that Dorset winter architecture must have depended heavily on snow, since there are so few remains of dwellings made from heavier materials. If the Palaeo-Eskimos did invent the domed snow house, its adoption by the Inuit would probably have been inevitable. Such a structure would have provided the newcomers with an efficient means of living and travelling in areas to which their Alaskan-based technology denied them access, and may have given them the necessary means for supplanting the originators of the structure.

Other possibilities for Dorset cultural survivals are either relatively minor – such as the appearance of a particular harpoon head style that seems to be based on a Dorset pattern – or are based on very little evidence. The complex of artifacts associated with Inuit dogsleds, for example – harness swivels, line buckles, whips, and so on – first appears at about the time that the Thule Inuit swept east across Arctic Canada. The flat-decked kayaks of the eastern Arctic Inuit are built in a different manner from those of Alaskan Eskimos, and it has been suggested that these modifications may be due to Dorset influence, yet we know practically nothing of Palaeo-Eskimo kayak construction or use. In a similar way, it seems possible that certain elements of the language or mythology or music of the Inuit, which differ somewhat from those of Alaskan Eskimos, may contain survivals of the earlier Palaeo-Eskimo cultural tradition. The existence of such survivals, however, is very difficult to detect and impossible to prove.

Anthropologists have even suggested that certain local groups in Arctic Canada and Greenland were remnants of a surviving Dorset population. Among these were the Sagdlermiut of Southampton Island in northern Hudson Bay, a small local group that died of an epidemic at the beginning of the twentieth century, and the Angmassalik people living on the barren southeastern coast of Greenland. Both the Sagdlermiut and Angmassalik were isolated from neighbouring Inuit groups, either because of geography or out of choice, and both had developed unique local cultural traits. Yet the cultures of both groups were firmly based in the Inuit tradition, and there is little reason to think of them as remnant Dorset people.

It now seems certain that no viable Palaeo-Eskimo population has flourished anywhere in Arctic North America within the past five centuries. After 3,000 years of enduring the harshest climatic conditions ever inhabited by humans and developing a remarkable cultural and artistic tradition, the Palaeo-Eskimos and their world had died. Yet this unique world did not disappear from history without leaving any trace. To the Inuit who inherited the Arctic, the Palaeo-Eskimos almost certainly contributed some small component of heredity. From the memories of stolen wives and adopted orphans, some minor elements of the Dorset language, culture, and view of the world may have been incorporated into those of the Inuit people. The domed *igloo,* that unique icon of Inuit culture, may be a surviving legacy of the Dorsets.

To the rest of the world, the Palaeo-Eskimos have given far more than the hundreds of pieces of art recovered by archaeology and the evidence of human ingenuity and endurance on the most distant margins of the habitable world. Their most valuable legacy lies in the realization that these two things occurred together and were part of the same phenomenon. The Palaeo-Eskimos provide an example of lives lived richly and joyfully amid dangers and insecurities that are beyond the imagination of the present world.

Note on Sources

The literature of Arctic history is widely scattered. Most publications take the form of academic articles, thinly dispersed through an array of journals devoted to archaeology, anthropology, and Arctic studies. These articles are communications among scholars in a specialized field and deal with specific and limited aspects of the subject. Readers who wish to sample this literature could look most profitably in the North American periodicals *American Antiquity, Arctic, Arctic Anthropology, Canadian Journal of Archaeology, Études Inuit/Inuit Studies,* and in the Danish journal *Folk.*

The majority of books on the subject are in the form of scholarly monographs. These are extended versions of papers such as those noted above, usually providing detailed reports on the archaeological materials recovered from individual sites or local regions. One of the best examples is also one of the more recent. *Crossroads to Greenland,* by Peter Schledermann (Calgary: Arctic Institute of North America 1990), presents and interprets the results of several years of archaeological effort on Ellesmere Island in the High Arctic and also provides an extensive bibliography of publications relating to the Palaeo-Eskimos. The Mercury Series of the Canadian Museum of Civilization and the Danish series Meddelelser om Grønland contain a number of similar monographs ranging over the past three decades.

Eskimo Prehistory, by H.G. Bandi (Fairbanks: University of Alaska Press 1969), and *The Eskimos and Aleuts,* by Don E. Dumond (London: Thames and Hudson 1987), offer a broader perspective. Both are textbooks dealing with the prehistory of Arctic peoples; both contain more archaeological detail than most readers would wish, concentrate on the prehistory of Alaska, and are somewhat out of date. A more fascinating introduction to the subject can be found in *Ancient Men of the Arctic,* by James L. Giddings (New York: Knopf 1967). This account of Arctic prehistory is presented in the form of an autobiography describing a lifetime's work in the field, and it conveys a sense of excitement and intellectual adventure that is sadly missing from most academic publications. *Arctic,* the fifth volume of the *Handbook of North American Indians* (Washington: Smithsonian Institution 1984), contains a number of useful summary articles on Arctic prehistory and is an excellent bibliographical reference.

The archaeology of Arctic Canada is treated on a general level in two books. *Prehistory of the Eastern Arctic,* by Moreau S. Maxwell (Orlando: Academic Press 1985), is a university-level text containing a great deal of detailed information on all aspects of the history and cultures of the Palaeo-Eskimos and Inuit. Robert McGhee's *Canadian Arctic Prehistory* (Hull: Canadian Museum of Civilization 1990) is written for a more general audience and is a smaller, illustrated handbook on the subject.

A discussion of published sources on Palaeo-Eskimos would not be complete without mentioning a few miscellaneous publications that are difficult to find but provide important insights into the subject and are well worth the search. Diamond Jenness's original report on the identification of the Dorset culture, is one such publication; it appeared under the title 'A New Eskimo Culture in Hudson Bay' in *The Geographical Review* 15 (1925):428-37. Another is 'The Silent Echoes: Prehistoric Canadian Eskimo Art,' in *The Beaver* 298 (1967):32-47. This article takes the form of a discussion between archaeologist William E. Taylor Jr. and art historian George Swinton and remains the classic source of ideas related to Palaeo-Eskimo art. Eigil Knuth's *Archaeology of the Musk-Ox Way,* Contributions de Centre d'Études Arctiques et Finno-Scandinaves no. 5 (Paris: Sorbonne 1967), describes the discovery of the Independence culture of far northern Greenland and develops stimulating interpretations of this early Palaeo-Eskimo way of life. The best example of early non-archaeological methods for the reconstruction of Arctic history is H.P. Steensby's *An Anthropogeographical Study of the Origins of the Eskimo Culture,* Meddelelser om Grønland 53 (Copenhagen: Commission for Scientific Research in Greenland 1916). This classic study takes us back to the beginnings of historical research in the Arctic and introduces the term Palaeo-Eskimos for the first time. The Palaeo-Eskimo concept was developed further in Helge Larsen and Froelich Rainey's *Ipiutak and the Arctic Whale Hunting Culture,* Anthropological Papers no. 42 (New York: American Museum of Natural History 1948). This monograph on an important North Alaskan excavation provides an interesting historical perspective on Arctic archaeology, as well as describing one of the most fascinating archaeological collections known from the Arctic world. The art of the Ipiutak people hints at relationships to Dorset art on the one hand and to that of imperial China on the other. A few minutes spent in looking through the photographs of Ipiutak burial masks and complex ivory carvings representing fantastic animals is a sure means of being captured by the fascination of the Palaeo-Eskimos and their world.

Index

Cooking, 62-4; in Dorset longhouse settlements, 207
Copper: tool-making, 202, 221
Copper Inuit, 53, 124
Coppermine River, 88, 89, 90-1, 202
Crampons, 130, 132
Crantz, David, 13
Cree, 176
Crystal: tool-making, *Plate 3*

D'Anglure, Bernard Saladin, 150
Dating, 16; Independence culture, 66-71; radiocarbon, 17, 37, 67, 73, 188
Deltaterrasserne, 30-2, 37
Denbigh Flint Complex, 29-30, 34, 175, 178
Dene, 116; contact with Palaeo-Eskimos, 78, 93, 102, 188-91; lands, 177
Devon Island, 103
Disease: introduced by Inuit, 223-4
Dogs, 145, 229
Dogsleds, 145-7; Inuit, 195, 223, 233
Dorset people, 25, 26, 27, 116-18, 120, 175; abandonment of drills, 142-4, *Plate 4;* artistic traditions, 149-56; belief system/world view, 142-4, 148, 156-8, 171-3, 204; bow and arrow, 144-5; burial methods, 147; clothing, 162, *Plate 2;* cultural survival of, 231-4; disappearance of, 210-13, 215, 231-4; dogsleds, 145-7; dwellings, 130-1, 133, 204-10; encounter with Inuit, 135, 145, 211, 213-29; Greenland, 191-4; Groswater, 129; Late Dorset period, 200-34; religion/shamanism, 154-7; Thule culture and, 184-8, 213-29; tool making, 136-45, 179; trade, 138-40, 148
Driftwood, 110, 140; carvings, 151, 160; tool handles, 142, 143
Drills, 230; abandonment of by Dorset people, 142-4, *Plate 4*
Drive lanes, 114-15, 144
Drums, 171; frames, 152, 153
Dundas Island, 206
Dwellings, 80; Chukchi, 43; climate changes affecting, 116; domed snow house (igloo), 232, 233; Dorset, 130-1, 133, 204-10; heating, 50-4, 116, 131; Independence people, 37-40, 48-54, 61-2, 63, 67; Inuit, 48; longhouses, 176, 207-10; Norse colonies, 192-3, 210; number per community, 204; tent, 37-40, 48-54, 61-2, 63, 67, 206; use of snow, 206, 232

Economic life, 10; High versus Low Arctic, 72
Eirik the Red, 191
Ekalluk River sites, 114-15
Ellesmere Island, 68, 70, 103, 128
Eskimo origins: early theories, 12-23; and Palaeo-Eskimos, 183-4; theory of European origins, 12-16
Eskimos: depiction of, 15; distinguished from Inuit, 5; European contact with, 12; language, 5, 13; relation to Palaeo-Eskimos, 183-4, 233
Eurasian peoples: dwellings, 37; relation of Palaeo-Eskimos to, 34-41

Falcon: Dorset carving, 165, 166-7, *Plate 14*
Family: disasters affecting, 125-6, 145; Inuit society, 122-3; Palaeo-Eskimo, 123-6
Famine, 107. *See also* Starvation
Fifth Thule Expedition, 20-3, 24
Fish: carvings of, 167-8
Fishing, 55, 70, 88; weirs, 135, 198-9, 211. *See also* Whales, hunting
Flint: chipped, 17, 28, 31, 37, 48, 129, 178, 190; Denbigh Complex, 29-30, 34, 175, 178; Independence people, 60
Food: storage, 61, 65, 92, 107, 125. *See also* Cooking; Hunting
Forest fires, 115
Fox traps, 212
Frobisher, Martin, 13, 15
Fuel, 50-4, 64. *See also* Heating

Rasmussen, Knud, 20, 203, 211
Reindeer, 16, 178
Religion: Dorset people, 154-6; shamanism, 155-6. *See also* Shamanism
Rivendell site, 70, 128
Ross, John, 12
Rowley, Graham, 150

Saami people, 13, 37, 38
Sagdlermiut people, 233
Saglek Bay, 190
Saqqaq people, 104, 128
Sculpin, 168
Sea ice environments, 131; carvings of animal life, 167-8, 169; coastal ice-hunting, 98-9, 111-14, 117-18, 120-1, 125-6, 146-7, 197; effect of climate change on, 111-14, 117, 125-6, 196-7, 200. *See also* Dorset people; Polynia
Seal: carvings, 167; hunting, 17, 80, 98, 111-14, 117-18, 129
Settlements, 8, 11; Barren Grounds, 88-92; Bering Strait, 186-7; Dorset longhouse, 207; Groswater Bay, 129; size of, 204-6; tent ring sites, 48-50, 67. *See also* Camps; Dwellings
Shaman-artists, 154-6, 160-1
Shamanism, 154-6, 170-3; amulets, 203-4, 205, 220, 226; drums, 171; healing, 170-1; 'helping spirits,' 157, 164, 202-3, 226; place of animals in, 157-8
Siberian peoples, 178; expansion of to Alaska, 73-80; hunting, 76; relation of Palaeo-Eskimos to, 34-43
Site visibility, 47, 71-2
Skeletons, 41
Sled shoes, 130, 132
Smoking Hills, 85, 86-7, 96, 157
Snow house. *See* Igloo
Social organization: band assemblies, 122, 126, 207; family, 122-6; group size, 123; Inuit society, 121-3; number of bands, 123
Southampton Island, 233

Spirit helpers, 157, 164, 226
Spiritual life: artifact record of, 10. *See also* Dorset people, belief system/world view; Shamanism
Starvation, 125-6, 128, 145, 197, 203, 231
Steensby, H.P., 20, 23, 30, 31, 33
Stone Age peoples: technologies, 8, 30, 34, 48
Stone lamps, 128, 130
Swinton, George, 152-5

Tartars: theory of Eskimo origins, 12-13
Tattooing, 78, 149-50, 159, 160, *Plate 8*
Taylor, William E., 152
Technology: early Alaskan, 178; Inuit, 223, 229; of Old versus New worlds, 25, 34, 41, 102, 188; relation to belief system, 142-4; Stone Age peoples, 8, 30, 34, 48. *See also* Artifacts; Tools; Weapons
Tent ring sites, 48-50, 67. *See also* Camps; Dwellings
Thule culture, 20-3, 24-5, 29, 184-8, 195, 213-33. *See also* Inuit
Time line, archaeological cultures in North America, 22
Tools: burins, 34, 48, 129; chipped-stone, 17, 28, 31, 37, 48, 129, 178, 190; drilling methods, 142, *Plate 4;* hafting techniques, 140, 143; Inuit, 48-50, 145, 195; materials for, 9, 60, 138-40, 190, 201-2, *Plate 3;* microblades, 34, 36, 48, 140; needles, 41, 59-60, 128-9, 142; Small Tool tradition, 37, 138; snow knives, 130, 232; stone-cutting, 9, 34; style and design of, 9, 128-30, 200-1; wood, 9, 60. *See also* Artifacts; Weapons
Trade: in Alaska, 184; Labrador, 189-90, 194; with Norse, 194; of tool-making materials, 138-40, 148
Tree line, 6, 78, 79, 110, 115, 196
Tuck, James, 190
Tundra, 78, 79, 84; climate changes and, 111; site visibility and, 71-2